"**Kenneth M. Mosley** is o1 long time. In this book, he g1 revelations to unlock mysteries sand times. Forget what you thought it meant to "**be fruitful and multiply**" and allow this book to expose new truths behind God's Word."
—Paula White

"Insightful and well-written, *Be Fruitful & Multiply* is loaded with wisdom for anyone, regardless of age, who's dedicated to pursuing their life's purpose. **Kenneth M. Mosley** has given us keys that unlock the destinies and dreams that lie within each of us."
—Dr. Ronn Elmore, The Relationship Doctor

"*Be Fruitful & Multiply* is packed with solid principles and motivational truths. Don't miss these practical keys to maximizing your life!"
—Dr. Suzan "Sujay" Johnson Cook, President, Hampton
University Ministries' Conference, Author, *Too Blessed to Be Stressed*

"**Kenneth M. Mosley** has an impressive way of challenging us to blaze the path God has set for our lives. *Be Fruitful & Multiply* will inspire you to disregard your past failures and reach for a bright, successful future."
—Gerard Henry, Host, BET's *Lift Every Voice*

"If you are seeking a life of abundance and impact, **Kenneth M. Mosley** lays out a God-centered formula to get you there."
—Valorie Burton, best-selling author of *Listen to Your Life*, *Rich Minds, Rich Rewards* and *What's Really Holding You Back?*

"Outstanding insight into prosperity as God intends it. Clearly God has given Ken a message the entire church should hear; enabling him to put forward in a practical and easily understood manner. This book is a must for every believer serious about maximising the covenants of promise where prosperity is concerned."
—Dr. Albert Odulele, Pastor, Glory House, London UK

Be Fruitful & Multiply

by
Kenneth M. Mosley

authorHOUSE™

1663 LIBERTY DRIVE, SUITE 200
BLOOMINGTON, INDIANA 47403
(800) 839-8640
WWW.AUTHORHOUSE.COM

First published by AuthorHouse 08/09/05

ISBN: 1-4208-7147-1 (sc)

Printed in the United States of America
Bloomington, Indiana

This book is printed on acid-free paper.

One Focus Communications
PO Box 201193
Arlington, TX 76006
www.KennethMosley.com

Dedication

To the Skipper, His Missionary and Their Tribe—
You helped your "little buddy" through some very tough years.
I am *very* grateful.

To the ONE, who gave me this message. May it reach and do all that You
intended. Thanks for choosing me.

Contents

Acknowledgments

I feel so honored to have so many people around me who have given me support and strength in some way. So many of you have just been added to my life in the last five years or so, but I know that God gave us to each other at just the right time. I am blessed, you are blessed, we are blessed! To my family: Mom and Dad, brothers, Kevin and Donavan, we are the Mosleys! I'm thankful that God chose you to shape my life. A big shout out to my cousin Anitra ("Artina") L. Walker (and the Ya-Yas!). Many of the final words of this book were written in your blue room. Thanks for all you've done for me. Much love.

To my New Mexico family: the Walker bunch, Kisha, Regina, the Phillips, the Terrells, the Reaves, the Jaynes, the Nowlins, the Adkins, Aunts Vera and Verna and on and on…there are too many to name! You have all helped me in so many ways, I can't put it all into words, but God knows and God bless!

To my New Mexico church family, the New Hope Church. To Bishop & Pastor Nina Cooper, from ushering to children's church to directing the youth, young adult and gospel choirs, I'm proud to be a son in your ministry. Thanks for teaching me to finish strong and start fresh, and thanks for every opportunity to unleash my gifts in your ministry. Also to Pastors L'Keith and Roz Jones of the Metropolitan Church in ABQ.

To a great group of guys whom I believe God has allowed to become brothers: to the Right Reverend Nolan E. Williams Jr., Superintendent Cornelius C. Clark, Big Brother Mark (and Dr. Jill!) Jones, Elder Timothy Charles (and Ms. Juliette) Ross, Rev. Marcus (and Lucy) Goodloe and Elder Michael A. (and Missionary Kimberly!) Mack. You don't know how each of you has provided immeasurable strength to me in troubled times. God has so much in store for each of you—just for blessing me.

To dear friends Scott Corbin, Jason Wade and Brad Keith. Wow. So when's the next time I'll see any of you??

To God's Leading Ladies who have crossed my path: Dawn Williams, Kim Rutherford, Brenda McClure, Verna Hamilton, Darcie Davis, Tracie Henderson, Sara Saavedra, Virginia Marshall, Elder Deborah Wheeler and Mother Jessie Mosley. Uniquely gifted and wonderfully made. I'm blessed to see each of you shine in the light of God's love. God bless.

To Angela DePriest, David Yeazell, Kevin G. Mosley, Carla M. Williams, Carolyn Miller, Tina Polite, Anitra Walker, Esme' Wemberly, Cesar Cedillo, Judie Dwyer and anyone else who contributed to this project. Your time and talent are not taken for granted.

To The Potter's House family: the Blues, the Silverbergs, the Alcorns, the Logans, and the Ellises. You have all been a particular blessing to me. A special thanks to the ministerial department of The Potter's House, Pastor Faison and particularly to MY elders: Elder and Minister Lionel and Emma Davis. You have fed me inside and out! Thank you for your wisdom and example.

To Dale Hill, Gerald Robinson and Elder Silas Wheeler: thanks for your support and example.

To Elder Jessie and Mary Washington: your story is a blessing, and you are an example of how to endure hardship as a good soldier. May your journey by faith take you further than you've ever dreamed. God bless.

To The Potter's House School of Ministry (PHSOM) and its overseeing pastor and dean, Rev. Dr. Rita L. Twiggs and Elder Sandra Jackson, esq. I know, I know, "It's in the BOOK!" So I'll just pray awhile…

To the Senior Associate Pastor Lawrence Robinson and the entire pastoral staff of The Potter's House: each of you has contributed something special to my experience. Particularly to Pastors Guynes, Meyers and Twiggs: thank you for the time you spent imparting "some good thing" to me. I'll always prize the time you've given to me.

To the mighty TV department of The Potter's House…great and lofty words cannot give you your deserved "props." So I'll just say "KUDOS!"

To Pastor Paula White, Dr. Ronn Elmore, Dr. Myles Munroe, Dr. Albert Odulele, Dr. Suzan Johnson-Cook, Valorie Burton, Gerard Henry, Bishop Alfred A. and Co-Pastor Susie C. Owens, Pastor Donnie McClurkin, Kirk Franklin, CeCe Winans, the late Pastor Amos & Mrs. Annie Sanders and to every great man and woman of God who have contributed to this book through wisdom, vision and motivation through an interview, a message, or otherwise, thank you for accepting the call and giving me strength to walk into mine.

Finally, and most definitively not least, to my pastor, Bishop T. D. Jakes. God used you to revive me, push me and shake me back into life. It's a pleasure, an honor and a challenge to sit under such great leadership. I really feel like I grew up (actually, I did) in your ministry. It's also been my pleasure to be a part of the (make-believe) T. D. Jakes School of Public Speaking! I admire you and respect you. To (Mrs.!) First Lady Jakes, you are so gracious and graceful. Thanks for being you and for extending me grace and kindness. It will not be forgotten.

To you, the reader. I've spent years writing (and living) this book. And really, I've learned from it and encouraged myself through the words God gave me. I only pray it helps you half as much.

Foreword

Volumes have been written on fruitfulness and multiplication, but Ken Mosley brings fresh and new insight to the subject. These all-time truths have been presented in a precise and practical way, and clearly *Be Fruitful & Multiply* is both thought provoking and heart searching.

I recommend this book to every believer with a desire to firmly grasp the principles, purposes and power of fruitfulness and multiplication. I reckon it ranks amongst the classics written by the faith giants of our time; there is more to the plot than amassing pounds and dollars for personal gain.

Get ready and get started! Here is a book with balanced and wholesome theology but presented in a manner that reaches out to the pulpit and pew alike. Ken's use of contemporary examples, easily understood illustrations and simple language brings the message home to the average twenty-first-century reader.

To Ken I say thank you for allowing your passion to see believers walk closer to the Lord and experience His refining fire come through. This book clearly demonstrates your times and seasons of dwelling in the Word and the presence of God. Each page unveils God's unfolding plan for man; from the cradle of conversion to the maturity of the cross.

Be Fruitful & Multiply contends that if you have embraced the school of thought that faith overrules and precludes you from trials and tribulations, be prepared for a rude awakening. Ken shows from the Scriptures and personal testimonies that faith equips the believer to come through challenges stronger than they went in.

Read this book and take a closer look at the purpose of your existence.

Evaluate how well you are engaged in your divine assignment. My personal encounters with the Lord give credence to how important this is. Eternity fast approaches, and many believers are unprepared to face it.

For the daring, God-pursuing and devil-chasing Christian; get ready for a change as you flip from one page to the next.

Dr. Albert Odulele
Glory House, UK

Introduction

I didn't really mean to write this book. I wasn't trying to write a book at all. I was studying for my *final* final exam at Southern Methodist University when the Holy Spirit spoke clearly to me. He interrupted my studying and began to speak to me about something completely unrelated to the subject I was cramming for. I thought, *I know You know I'm studying, so can we discuss this later?*

Well, I didn't hesitate to grab one of my journals. The information was coming so fast, I had to rush and begin writing it as it came to me. It's a feeling similar to watching a file download. One moment you're waiting; the next moment, the whole file is there, pages and pages, displayed on your computer monitor. The concept, the meaning of life, there it was, downloaded from my inner man into my conscious. It was extraordinarily profound, so much so that I was shocked at what He told me. And so I asked Him to prove it in His Word, and He did.

What came from that encounter was an idea that I hadn't heard presented in the way I had that night. From there came lessons in the Word of God, supporting concepts, and then, of course, tests. I guess, looking back, it was only fitting that the Lord interrupt my studying, something so finite, to impart to me something so infinite, for which I would and still am being tested.

On the following pages are portions of what He showed me about my life, and about accessing its plans and the purpose. I was at a point of utter confusion in my life, and really needed a rhema word of revelation from God. I didn't know just what I needed, but of course He did. He told me, and continues to tell me, about His plan for my life…and He continues to show me, by the path that my life has taken.

As you read these pages, I pray that you'll be refreshed, renewed, and restored to the point that God can move you from a desolate, barren place to one of fruitfulness: bearing fruit, to more fruit, to much fruit. It is possible to be fruitful and multiply, just as the Bible says.

Please digest this material in the spirit in which it was given to me. I am not the Authority; God is. I'm just someone who wants to share some things he's been taught by the Master Teacher.

I'm learning, just like you, that it is not God's will that our lives be wasted. He wants us to be productive, fruitful people. I'm on my way, just like you, and together we'll make it! You and I, we will be fruitful and we will multiply!

Kenneth M. Mosley

Part I

🌀 Fruit 🌀

The Mission

"So here it is...my first book and I'm a little nervous. I mean, after all, me? A writer? I'm probably more shocked than anyone else: my family, friends and even you, the reader. But that's just how it is with God. He puts something deep down inside of you, virtually hidden, until just the right time. And then, like a time-sensitive bomb, out of nowhere, it just explodes!"

It's just got to come out sooner or later. What is it? It's simple really. It's...your mission.

The First Thing
He Told Me

⟪ *Genesis 1:28* ⟫

SO, THERE I WAS STUDYING FOR FINAL exams and the Lord interrupted my study session.

He said, "The first instructions I gave to man were to be fruitful and multiply." It was just like that. There was no "stop what you're doing for a moment; I have something to say."

He just kind of said it, and I stopped. I looked up, and then I tried to resume my studies.

"So what do you suppose that means?"

I answered, "I thought the first commandment was for children to obey their parents."

"That's the first commandment with promise, but the first instructions were to be fruitful and multiply."

A little skeptical, I replied, "If this is really God, show me what you're talking about."

"Go to Genesis."

Sure enough, there it was, before the first chapter even ended, 'be fruitful and multiply.'

I actually learned this principle from the late Kenneth Hagin. My grandfather was a correspondence student and graduate from Rhema Bible College. So consequently and thankfully, I have been inundated with teachings of faith and the Holy Spirit ever since I can remember. One thing I learned from "Dad" Hagin is that if you hear a concept or teaching, whether from someone else or in your own spirit, and you're not sure it is of God, there will *always* be a scriptural revelation of it. All you have to do is ask the Holy Spirit to show it to you in the Word of God, and He will.

So I employed that principle here. Now, of course I had heard this scripture tons of times before. I had always thought that it meant for Adam and Eve to have plenty of children because they were the only people on earth.

But that night, I learned that that scripture means much more than I had supposed.

At first, that phrase almost sounds like three repetitions of the same instruction. "Be fruitful, and multiply, and replenish the earth…" Now wait a minute. Was God being redundant? God never wastes anything, including words. So what did He mean?

Again He asked me, "So what do you suppose that means?"

"It means that Adam and Eve should have lots of kids, so the earth would be full of people."

Well, I was right, and I was wrong. Here's what the Lord showed me.

Yes, Adam and Eve were supposed to have plenty of children; that's why God told them to replenish the earth. He was talking about physical things, not only because He stated the location of earth, but also because He goes on to list how they would replenish and subdue the earth. He institutes the seed principle in the following verses, and tells the first humans how living things operate.

So, yes, husbands and wives should reproduce. But there was still that matter of being fruitful and multiplying. One thing that I noticed about Genesis 1:28 is what it first says: "And God blessed them."

Now this is important to understand, because if we're not careful, we'll miss its real meaning and just lump it in with all of the physical talk that follows.

John 4:24 tells us something important about God. Most Christians know it already, and we believe it. We see it in Genesis, but it's so plain and definitive in John. "God is a spirit." So in Genesis when it reads that God created man in His image (Genesis 1:27), we have to know that the image spoken of here is a spiritual image.

When I was growing up, we used to attend Sunday school every Sunday morning. And the teachers would tell us that God created us in His image. And because God is not ugly, no one else is ugly either. That's a sweet thing to say, but it dilutes an important truth of God's Word. When God created us, He made us to look and to be like Him. Just like we look like our earthly parents and have some of their mannerisms and tendencies, our spiritual appearance should be like that of our heavenly Father.

God is a spirit! So when He blessed man and woman, He did so with a spiritual blessing. We always think of blessings as cars, houses, land, and other material things, but those aren't blessings. Those are products of the blessing. The blessing was the ability, power, and favor God gave you to get those things. The blessing is the talent to work the job that He gave you to get those things. Blessings aren't physical things. They come from a spiritual God. Even if they manifest themselves as physical things, blessings are spiritual, and they come with a spiritual assignment. The apostle Paul tells us that God has already blessed us with all *spiritual blessings* in heavenly places (Ephesians 1:2). And blessings always have a purpose.

He blessed them, and immediately gave them an assignment. And with a spiritual blessing, He gave a spiritual assignment. "Be fruitful and multiply."

Now, reproduction means using the seed placed inside of you from your previous generations and making another copy. This principle is shown in verse 24 when God made the living creatures. Every living thing has its own seed and creates after its own kind.

We were made in God's likeness. In other words, we were created after His kind.

So when God blessed man and woman and told them to be fruitful and to multiply, He was specifically talking about multiplying after our kind, which is His kind—the God kind.

Remember, God is a Spirit. We were created in His likeness. That means that *we are spirits*. We live inside bodies, but ultimately, we are spirits. And when we reproduce, we reproduce spiritually, first, then physically.

Now if you're thinking, *Well that was just what He told the first man and woman. That doesn't apply to me*, think again. It absolutely applies to you. He blessed them, then gave them the command to "be fruitful and multiply, and to replenish the earth."

> *When God blessed man and woman and told them to be fruitful and to multiply, He was specifically talking about multiplying after our kind, which is His kind— the God-Kind.*

They did. They replenished the earth, and we are still a part of that replenishment. And because they reproduced after their own kind, they passed on their characteristics to us. We have the blessing God gave Adam and Eve, and we have the command to be fruitful and multiply.

The theological law of first mentioned means that the first mention of a thing, concept, or idea is the model that every other mention of the same thing, concept, or idea should follow.

So when God gave this instruction to man as the concept for his job in life, every man from Adam on was given the same instruction. After all, if the laws of reproduction are true, Adam was the carrier of the seed of all mankind. The Scriptures tell us that when he fell into a sinful state, all mankind fell with him. And if we all fell with him, we were inside of him when God gave him life's first instructions.

Are you still doubtful that these instructions don't apply to us today? After God flooded the earth and spared only Noah's family, He gave them the same instructions in Genesis 9:1. Same God, same instruction, and even though it was given to a different man, man (Noah *and* his sons) had the same orders.

We are here for a purpose. God doesn't waste anything, and He certainly doesn't waste life. So look at it this way: the first thing God told you was to *be fruitful and multiply*. It's your mission, it's your main goal, and it's your destiny.

Now what is the fruit, how do we multiply it, and with whom do we do so? These are all very good questions. Keep reading.

It's All Inside!

◈ *Genesis 1:11–13; Genesis 2:6–7* ◈

WE'VE BEEN CALLED TO BE FRUITFUL, but many of us have no idea where to begin the mission of manifesting fruit. While we've looked for people, places, and things to be the beginning and end of the search for our purpose, there's really only one place where we should begin and end our quest for fulfillment in God's kingdom. The first and actually quite simple truth is this: *it's all inside!*

The power, reason, motivation, strength, and resources that you need to be fruitful and multiply are inside of you! So many times, though, we don't realize just how powerful we are. Our fleshly insecurities and our unhealthy self-images stop us from realizing who we are in God's eyes.

But Genesis 1:11–13 takes our mind off of our own shortcomings and places our mission in view. This passage is to be a template for any believer with purpose. We're told to be fruitful, so why not take a moment to look at one of the fundamentals of how fruit is produced? In these verses, God says the tree yields fruit after its kind and that *its seed is in itself!*

Its seed is in itself! We already know that a tree yields fruit that's just like it. And if we're told that we are to produce fruit, then that means that we must first recognize that we *are* the fruitfulness of God!

Genesis 1:26 and 2:7 give us more insight. God said, "Let us make man in our own image and after our likeness (or *kind*)." Then, we're told that God breathed the breath of life *into* man!

I believe that the breath of life is that seed placed within us for future fruit production and multiplication. God is so sovereign—powerful and in charge— that when He told man that he was to replenish the earth, God had already made preparation for the fall of man. He knew that sin would separate Him from man, so He made it our assignment to replenish the earth of what it lacked: His presence!

Well, how do we do that? We do it with the seed that's inside of us. Deep down on the inside of you is the Spirit of God. His Spirit or breath (or divine inspiration) is really in every man, but, because of sin, it's dormant in many people. But Jesus showed us by His resurrection that it is possible to be dead in sin at one point of life, but be resurrected in life through the power and Spirit of God at another time.

And it is the revived, renewed Spirit of God that lives inside of me, giving me resurrected life and power!

Personally, I'm thankful that it is by grace through faith that I receive salvation (Ephesians 2:8). It is a gift from God, and there's not a thing I can do to earn it. I just have to receive the grace God's given me. Then, realizing that there's nothing good in my carnal man (otherwise known as my flesh), I have to continually receive His grace to live how He wants me to live.

And really, that's the key to fruitfulness. The best part of fruit is not the skin, or the fleshly covering; it's the delicious taste that pours out from inside. And the best part is that once fruit has been digested, there's still a way that we can get more of the same fruit that we love. It's through the seed that's inside of it!

It is the seed of God's Spirit that's inside of us. And it's His seed that He wants to come out from behind the walls of our flesh and be placed in the earth to produce more fruit after its kind. And *its* kind is really *His* kind! So our purpose is to take what He's placed in us—His Spirit—and allow those around us to receive it.

Now every fruit has its own distinct taste, appearance, and benefit to the body. That's true, but there are also certain qualities that are consistent in all fruit. So we can't look at the outward appearance or the differences of the gifts and talents in this case because the fruit we're to display is spiritual fruit.

We don't normally see spiritual things with our naked human eyes. But we can sense them with our own spirits. And the spiritual characteristic that we have all been called to display is the *heart of God.* That's all. It is God's heart.

We can get in touch with the heart and will of God through our connection to His Spirit, which is inside of us. Imagine that. The old saying is true; it *is* what's inside of us that counts. And if you've ever doubted your ability to do something significant for God, your doubts will subside as we travel further on this pathway to fruitfulness. But remember, in order for the seed to be planted in the ground, the flesh that's on the outside of it must become separated from the seed. This can happen by someone or something consuming its outer flesh, or by the flesh just decaying until there's nothing left but the inner seed.

> *Anything God expects or accepts comes to Him because of Him! That's why He put Himself inside of you!* ☺》

I believe that both happen in our lives. The environment in which we live, as well as the people around us, consume the parts of us that are most readily available to them. That's not always a bad thing either. People are interdependent and are meant to feed off of each other, and the healthiest way for this to happen is when we expose ourselves to the environment of the washing of the Word of God, so that we are clean and ready for consumption. Like it or not, if you're alive, you will affect the lives of others, so it's important that what they receive from you is clean and beneficial to their well-being. There are great, flavorful parts of our personality and personal make-up that God meant to feed the people closest to us.

But again, it's what's inside that counts! After we've given all that we can to others, what should be left with them is the seed of the Spirit of God, which drops into the ground of their soul, taking root and bearing the fruit of what God has placed within us. This is the beginning of cycles of generations, where, long after we're gone, the wisdom, love, hope, and encouragement that we've given to one person benefits an entire family or even a nation of people.

Even if only one person eats of our fruit during our own lifetime, it's comforting to realize that for ages after our decayed remains have dissolved into the face of this earth, there will be people who will enjoy the fruit inside the seed God planted within us.

I truly believe that some of the smaller things that we give to people, the things we feel that are insignificant, will be the things that grow into awesome trees for the kingdom of God. Those little blessings we give to people are just little seedlings that we will harvest on earth and in eternity.

We must realize how potent we are, and that it's the Spirit of God, the breath of life, that's within us that is the fruitful factor. Fruitful people need only rely on that spirit to lead them into the path of production and blessing. And on that path, we'll meet those who will fertilize, water, weed out, and mature us when we follow the Spirit that's inside of us.

Have you taken time to check out what's inside of you? Do you know that if God is powerful enough to create the world, then the Spirit of God that's inside of you has the same power? After all, we're made *like* Him! If He, in the person of His Son, Jesus, can perform awesome miracles and then say, "You'll do greater things than this," then you've got awesome, miracle-working power inside of you too (John 14:12)! Romans 11:33–36 tells us that God's wisdom, riches, and knowledge are beyond human comprehension, and that of Him, through Him, and to Him are all things. He can use anything for His own purpose and glory.

Anything God expects or accepts comes to Him because of Him! That's why He put Himself inside of you! So you don't have to pressure yourself, as if this thing called "life" depends on you. Your purpose, your calling, and your future all depend on Him—and He's inside of you!

The power to create, to be fruitful, and to multiply is within us. No matter the isolation, dilapidated surroundings, or lack of understanding from others, we can't use them as excuses to shy away from our call to greatness.

Remember: Greater is *HE* that's within us, than he that's in the world (1 John 4:4). He's inside of me, and I am His fruitful creation. And what's within must come out! Nurture, rely on, and unleash the Spirit of God that's within you, and you will be fruitful and multiply!

Fruit? What Fruit?

Psalm 8:5–6; John 15:7–8; John 17:4

WE KNOW THAT GOD has commanded us to be fruitful and to multiply. And if the fruit is not just childbearing, but it's also about God's Spirit within us, how do we go about doing that? Well, we took a look at the first man and woman, and we got our first instructions. But as we know, they fell from grace, so we may not want to solely look to them for answers on how to achieve the goals that God has set for us.

Instead, let's look at the Second Adam, and see how He accomplished His mission. We know Jesus as the Second Adam (1 Corinthians 15:22, 45–49) because He came to earth to restore us to the relationship we had with God. He brings us back into the relationship with God that the first Adam had before his fall into sin. Jesus repairs the breach that has divided us from our Father.

We know from John 1:14 that Jesus is God in the flesh. He became human, just like us. So we look at Him as our example of a godly man. Because He was a man, He had to face man's problems, and as our redeemer, He was confronted with temptation, just like we are (Hebrews 4:15). The difference is that Jesus beat the enemy every time! He had our issues to face, and He had our mission too. He, too, had to be fruitful and multiply.

In John 15:10, we see that as a human, Jesus had to carry out God's commandments, just as we have to. He carried out God's commandments, and He abided in His Father's love because He wanted to bear fruit. Here's what Jesus said:

"I am the vine; you are the branches. If a man remains in me and I in him, he will bear much fruit" (John 15:5).

So those who abide in the Father bear fruit. Now, it's easy to get confused. The entire Gospel of John is riddled with statements from Jesus announcing just how "God" He is. John is careful, even from the beginning of his book, to firmly establish the fact that Jesus is God. He's not just another prophet, but He is GOD in the flesh. That's why we worship Him and pray to Him, and not His mother Mary. She was a great woman and a highly favored vessel of God. But Jesus *was* God on the earth. Throughout John's Gospel, we'll see Jesus say, "I am…" and then He'll use the same phrase to describe God. He does this to show us that He is God in the flesh.

The same is true in this chapter of John. In John 15:10, we see the man Jesus noting His own obedience to His Father's will. And Jesus said that when we bear fruit, His Father is glorified (John 15:8). Simply put, the final product of the fruit that we're told to bear is the glory of God!

We are fruitful when the glory of God is seen in our lives. Now, what is the glory of God? It's more than the goose bumps you feel in a worship service. It's more than a shout or a praise. It's even more than the standard definition that we've heard as "the manifest presence of God."

The glory of God can be seen in all of these, but there is so much more to it than that.

When the word *glory* was used in the Old Testament, it symbolized the honor, splendor, renown, and strength that is associated with God. In the New Testament, the word takes on more meaning. It also includes the estimation or opinion in which one is held. It denotes the reputation, good standing, and esteem given to someone. And in the New Testament, the word for glory also includes the splendor, radiance, and majesty centered in Jesus.

At first glance, the meaning of the word *glory* seems to just be related to speaking nicely about a person. It does, but the word *glory* relates to more than just the thoughts of people. When we see the word *glory*, especially in the New Testament, it does relate to the way that people thought about Jesus, but only because of the works that He did! In other words, the *glory* that people saw and the high regard in which they esteemed Jesus was because of the signs, wonders, and miracles that He did.

In John 2:11, we see an example of this idea. It was after Jesus' first miracle, the turning of water into wine, that Jesus manifested God's glory, splendor, and majesty.

We esteem God, and give Him honor and glory because of who He is, but also because of what He's done! He has a great reputation with us because of all that He's done and is able to do. In Psalm 8:1, the psalmist speaks of God's glory, and then he goes on to list all that God has done, in heaven and on earth.

We know that we have produced fruit when God gets the glory. And God gets the glory when we allow Him to work through us to accomplish wonderful things. Like Jesus, we glorify God when the essence of who we are as *Christians*—those who bear the name, spirit, mind, and actions of Christ our Savior and Lord—is manifested in the things we do.

In John 11, Jesus' friend Lazarus dies. As Jesus goes to raise Lazarus from the dead, He assures his sisters that Lazarus's healing will not lead to death, but it will lead to the glory of God. Well, it seems that Lazarus dies. But Jesus, in His awesome power, works another miracle, and Lazarus is brought back to life. His healing was for the glory of God.

Jesus glorified God in bringing Lazarus back to life. When human beings do God things, they bear fruit and God gets the glory! We glorify Him in our acts, just as Jesus did.

But here's the catch: there is no glory without a miraculous story. And that's where the word *glory* has many uses in the Bible: the weight or strength of God, particularly in times of conflict and opposition. One of the reasons that the wonderful things that Jesus does are glorious (beautiful and splendid) is because of the not-nearly-as-glorious (beautiful and splendid) situations in which those things are done. In short, His glorious works of the impossible are always in stark contrast to the desperate and bleak state of affairs that were present.

> *When human beings do God things, they bear fruit and God gets the glory!* ◎〟

When the psalmist bragged about how glorious it was that God created the earth, it's because He was able to do so not just out of pure darkness but out of nothing at all! And the same is true in our own lives. Our advantageous situations and extraordinary demonstrations are only glorious when compared to the disadvantaged beginnings and ordinary makings of our lives. That's when it's most obvious that God's glory is what people are seeing.

This is the fruit we're called to bear, the glory of God on the earth. This glory defies natural circumstances. This glory overshadowed the birth of a baby in the substandard accommodations of a barn. This glory operates independently of either the praise or the mocking of men. And it's this glory that will be seen along the journey of our lives as we complete our purpose. And when we do, we can be as Jesus was, when He was soon to give His life for us on Calvary. John 17:4 tells us that we glorify God when we finish the work He has assigned us.

Each of us has the same assignment, to bear fruit, and thereby glorify God in the earth. But because we have many different talents and gifts, the way we accomplish this assignment varies. But one thing remains true: when we become fruitful, God gets all the glory!

Baby Steps to Bearing Fruit

≪ *John 14:23; 15:1–5* ≫

WE'VE LEARNED THAT BEARING FRUIT means bringing glory to God. We glorify God when we abide in Him. Now, for many people who have attended church for many years, sometimes much of John 15 is too familiar to have great significance.

We know the common definition of the word *abide*. It means to remain or to dwell. So what does Jesus really mean when He uses this term in John 15:4?

"Abide in me, and I in you. As the branch cannot bear fruit of itself, except it abide in the vine, no more can ye, except ye abide in me" (John 15:4).

Clearly, Jesus is saying here, "If you want to bear fruit, you can only do it with My help!" He's already explained in verse 1 that He is the vine, and we are the branches. This statement is critical to any child of God that wants to do anything great for the kingdom of God.

We may not all want to admit it, but there have been times for each of us when we had great intentions and great aspirations to do great things for God. But we went about it the wrong way. Many of us have had moments when we received a calling from the Lord to our purpose, and immediately went running! We didn't know where we were running to, or how we would get there, but we just began to run, making plan "A's" and plan "B's" without consulting God.

> *Our walk with God is predicated on our willingness to challenge life and persevere as we travel through these steps to accomplish all that He has assigned us.* ☺»

But at the beginning of the chapter, we hear from Jesus (remember, He's God in the flesh) telling His disciples that He is the vine, and that they (and all believers) are the branches. He tells us that we cannot bear fruit unless we abide with Him : "*Apart from me you can do nothing*" (John 15:5b).

The first thing that we must always remember is that we are only the *branches*. How many branches can live without being connected to the vine? Have you ever passed a branch that was lying on the ground with all of its leaves, and all of its fruit fresh and thriving? If you have, I guarantee that the next day, if that branch was still lying there, you didn't see the same things. The leaves would have lost some of their color, the fruit would begin to wither and rot, and the branch itself would become dried up and rotten.

That's just how we get sometimes. We forget that we can only bear fruit because of our connection to Christ. It's not enough just to receive a vision and a call from God to our purpose. If we don't pursue it the way He wants us to, we won't be productive.

And any branch that isn't productive is taken away (John 15:2). God would never expect us to do anything that isn't within our capacity. We *can* achieve the goal that God has set for, but we've got to do it His way! We must stay connected to the Vine if we want to bear fruit. We must abide in Him and He in us. This gives true meaning to the well-known Scripture that tells me that I can do all things through Christ who strengthens me (Philippians 4:13). We *can* do all things! And it's through the True Vine that we get strength to accomplish these things.

He is the Vine! Strength comes from the Vine! Life travels through the vine to the branches! Food and resources come from the vine to the branches! We can only be productive through our connection to the True Vine.

And remember, we have to connect with the *True* Vine. We can't just connect with any vine that looks and smells like the *True Vine*. Just because we go to church or can quote Scripture doesn't mean that we are connected to the True Vine. Remember, the enemy knows the Bible too! He tried to use it to manipulate Jesus during His time of tempting (Luke 4). So quoting Scripture definitely does not mean that we're connected to the True Vine.

Well, how do we know that we're connected to the True Vine? The answer is simple: you begin to bear fruit. Now, the process of bearing fruit is not quite as simple, but apparently God knows that, because Jesus shows us that there are steps to bearing fruit.

These phases bring the believer from bearing fruit, to bearing more fruit, and finally, to bearing much fruit. The Bible lists these phases of fruit bearing and they cannot be ignored. In the life of every believer, there is the capacity to do *some* things for God, to do *more* things for God, and to accomplish *great* things for Him. That's what these phases indicate. Our walk with God is predicated on our willingness to challenge life and persevere as we travel through these steps to accomplish all that He has assigned us. However, each step has a process. I believe the process is the same for each fruit-bearing phase. It's the intensity of each process that varies.

In fact, this book is designed with this concept in mind. As Christians knowing and understanding our purpose, I believe that we can bear fruit on very basic levels. Then, as we mature and overcome inward and outward obstacles, we bear more fruit. Finally, I believe that when we pursue a personal, intimate relationship with God, and begin to know Him on a level that surpasses what He does for and through us, we begin to bear much fruit for His kingdom and for His glory. The chapters that follow this are consistent with this line of thought. Let's take a look at each level of fruit bearing.

Fruit, More Fruit, and Much Fruit

❦ *John 15* ❦

THE FIRST STEP TO BEARING FRUIT on any level is what I call the preparation phase. We prepare to bear fruit by first making sure that the Father is abiding with us. John 14:23 gives instructions on how to do this.

"Jesus answered and said unto him, 'If a man love me, he will keep my words: and my Father will love him, and we will come unto him, and make our abode with him'" (John 14:23).

In order for us to abide in Jesus and for Him to abide in us, we have to keep His words. We keep His words because we love Him. Honestly, I've found that it is *so* much easier to "do the right thing" when I have an ongoing love relationship with the Lord. Unfortunately, it's easy to be a believer and not have a love relationship with Jesus. Some translations of John 14:23 (AMP) read that Jesus says, "If a person [really] loves me..." We have said for years that we love Him. But here, we clearly see that our love will provoke us into action. We'll obey His Word.

Actually, love *always* produces action. When God sent Jesus to the world to die for us, it was His love that provoked His action to do so (John 3:16). When Jesus was baptized, His act of submission to this symbolic rite of passage pleased God, causing a response from heaven: "This is my *beloved* son, in whom I am well pleased" (Matthew 3:17, emphasis mine). His obedience so pleased God that He sent His Holy Spirit, in the symbolic form of a dove, to *abide* and rest with Jesus (Matthew 3:16).

This is part of the first step to bearing fruit. Once our love for the Father draws us to Him in prayer and obedience, we provoke the Lord to come to us, and make His abode with us (John 14:23). When God abides with us, we have made the connection that causes us to begin to bear fruit.

Some of these first fruits come from the realization of the fact that we can ask what we will of the Lord, and it will be given to us because our love relationship with the Lord causes Him to act on our behalf, producing the fruit of answered prayer. As Jesus was about to be arrested before His crucifixion, He shared some important truths about love.

In John 16:24, Jesus tells the disciples that they can ask the Father anything in His name, and they would receive. But verses 26 and 27 struck my attention. He clarifies that when they (or anyone who believes in Him—and this includes us!) ask anything in Jesus' name, He won't be praying on our behalf, because the Father loves the disciples for loving Jesus. This is a GREAT truth!

Jesus told His disciples that they would receive what they're asking for from God because of His tender love for them. He loved them because they believed that Jesus was sent from God's side to the earth. It was His personal love for them that gave them the access and the ability to receive what they needed from God. Jesus said, "I don't even have to ask My Father for you. He loves YOU, and because He loves YOU, YOU can get what you need from Him when you ask Him yourself!"

Now, this doesn't mean that Jesus is not our High Priest; He still is. He does pray on our behalf (Hebrews 7:25), and the Holy Spirit prays through us (Romans 8:26) because we don't always know what to pray for. But for those things that we know to pray for, if we just believe and ask the Father, He will give it to us! There are certain desires that we have in our hearts, and the Lord longs to give them to us. There are people we pray for whom can be blessed by our association with the Lord. Our friends and families can be blessed because of our prayers on their behalf. We have an assurance that He hears us (1 John 5:14), because His love for us has gotten us access to Him that grants our requests.

I wonder what would happen if we began to pray with this revelation in mind? Our faith would soar, and we'd stop praying with one eye half-opened trying to see if anything will happen in our lives. We'd pray with the power and authority that is rightfully ours! We certainly didn't earn it, but Jesus, who is God in the flesh, said it's ours! It's our faith in and love for Jesus that has gotten us answers to prayer.

Now, this is not a "name it, claim it" theology. It's the Word of God. Jesus said that when we ask anything in His name, the Father will give it to us. This is not a manipulative, materialistic way to receive possessions either. We must realize that when we ask for something in Jesus' name, God honors our request as if Jesus is the person making the request. If we make a request that is out of the will of God, even if we attach an "in the name of Jesus" on the end of it, it can't be granted. The key to asking things in Jesus' name is the realization that Jesus prayed foremost that the will of God be done in every situation. Likewise, our requests are granted because asking in His name includes asking according to His will.

This is where our love relationship with Him is also advantageous. When we draw close to Him in prayer and in study of the Word of God, our prayers begin to resemble those that Jesus would pray. Therefore, we're not just adding some hocus pocus phrase on the end of the sentence. The phrase "in the name of Jesus" reminds us and it reminds God of the covenant or contract He has with us about our access to Him through the name of Jesus. Jesus told His disciples that no man can come to the father except through Him (John 14:6). And when we fall in love with Jesus, our love perpetuates a desire to want what He wants, and we pray prayers that are in agreement with His will for our lives. He took on our attributes of sin, so we could take on His attributes of power over sin, and sonship in the Lord. Our will becomes subject to His, and our prayers are plans of purpose leading our lives on the paths to bearing fruit.

Once we begin to bear fruit, we'll walk to the next stage of bearing fruit. But not before we begin another step called pruning. John 15:2 details this process. As we begin to bear fruit, the Lord, as any cultivator would, prunes the branches that are bearing fruit. He cuts parts of the branch to enable it to continue to bear fruit. Actually, the pruning process helps the believer to produce more fruit than before. One translation of verse 2 says that He "cleanses and repeatedly prunes every branch that continues to bear fruit, to make it bear more and richer and more excellent fruit."

The pruning process is never easy, and it's never a one-time occurrence.

Pruning involves cutting back, and cutting back is never painless. The Bible says that the wounds of a friend are faithful

The pruning process is never easy, and it's never a one-time occurrence.

(Proverbs 27:6), and the pruning process is part of the wounds we incur as believers. The Lord allows us to encounter certain situations because they will inevitably help us bear the fruit that is richer and more excellent than the fruit we first brought to bear. We can't just be satisfied with the preliminary fruit that we've seen in our lives. If we ever want to get to the final stage of fruit bearing, we have to experience pruning.

It's during the pruning process that the Lord shapes our character, sharpens our gifts, and purges our motives. We need pruning because the level of blessing that the Lord wants to give us requires responsibility on our part. The weight of glory that we receive can only be handled by developed spiritual muscles that can balance, lift, and endure great levels of success.

Before we decide that our pruning process needs to be shortened, we should ask ourselves some questions. Can I endure public criticism? Success always brings a certain amount of controversy (Mark 13:13). Is my walk with the Lord strong enough to endure failure? What are my motives for seeking success? Can I honestly say that I would choose God over large sums of money? Are my time-management, money-management, and prioritizing skills acceptable to God? Are my people and relationship-building skills sharpened enough to represent God well? Is my family life strong enough to support my success? Is my self-esteem healthy enough to properly handle the success God gives me, without misplacing my priorities or squandering the results of my success? Do I have the integrity it takes to manage the perceived power that success often brings? Is my relationship with God strong enough that I hear His voice, and follow His instructions, regardless of how good (or bad) an opportunity looks on the surface?

The Lord helps us answer these and more pruning questions as we take steps toward the last stage of fruit bearing.

Sometimes, it seems as if the pruning process is the longest stage in bearing fruit, but that's only because few people discuss the final stage.

The final stage of bearing fruit is the stage where there is much fruit. In this stage, our fruit remains, because the pruning process has caused the branches in our lives to bear the rich and lasting fruit that God intended. Once the believer bears much fruit, it's evident that the Lord is with him or her, and that they have followed, in some form, the proper steps to producing lasting, remaining fruit.

In the previous stages, however, there can be such darkness and turmoil that we're not sure just where we stand in the process. The pain of the pruning seems to be the only part of our lives that we're sure of, and we don't know if we'll ever see our fruit remain.

Honestly, I believe that some areas of our lives bear fruit, more fruit, and even much fruit quickly, and others require repeated pruning. But it's these areas that will yield the most fruit in our lives.

As we travel on this journey to bearing fruit, we'll discuss these stages and challenges in more depth, and together we'll begin to realize that God's will is for us to bear much fruit, and we can do it with His help! We can and we will bear much fruit!

Don't Take It With You

❦ *Matthew 21* ❧

KING DAVID'S WISE SON, Solomon, shares some important truths with us about bearing fruit. Ecclesiastes 3:1 tells us that everything has a season and a time and purpose under heaven. Everything that is under heaven's domain is activated by seasons. There is a set time for every activity under heaven. Solomon lists for us some of these activities: a time to live and a time to die; a time to weep and a time to laugh; a time to plant and a time to harvest what is planted.

Seedtime and harvest will always be around, as long as the earth remains, according to Genesis. That's why so much of the Bible uses agricultural symbols and connotations. Not only was farming the way that many people earned their living in biblical times, but the principles of sowing and reaping are in action when bearing the spiritual fruit that God commanded us to bear.

The fact of the matter is that God wants to harvest what He's planted inside of us. The first thing He planted inside of us was the breath of life. We are the only creatures that God created in which He breathed His own Spirit. That's why we're made in His image. And that's why the command to be fruitful and multiply far surpasses sexual reproduction. Any living thing can reproduce, but we've got a higher calling. To whom much is given, much is required (Luke 12:48). And we've been given much.

There's no way that we can be created in God's image and be mundane and mediocre! We've got God's breath on the inside of us! And because it's His breath on the inside of us, He knows exactly what we are capable of. There's no "I can't" with God; He knows that what's inside of you is powerful enough to frame the world. There's no way that "I can't" will ever be an excuse with Him.

Consider that! This is the person who spoke the entire universe into being. Then He breathed His breath into you and me. When we fell from perfection and grace, He made a way for us to be redeemed and restored back to our original condition. That means that we came back to the same state the first man and woman were in before the fall. We have the same creative power. We can name, create, and oversee things that God has assigned to us.

We've been given much, and God wants to see a return on the investment of His Spirit within us. In other words, He's planted the seed of His Spirit, anointing, and ability in our spirits, and He wants to harvest it.

This was the case in Matthew 21. Jesus was traveling from Bethany into Jerusalem and became hungry. It's interesting to note that while the name "Bethany" indicates a house of dates (fruit), it also indicates poverty and affliction in a root form, while "Jerusalem" means peaceful city. So, symbolically Jesus was traveling from a land of lack to a land where wholeness abounded.

Between these two places, He sees a fig tree that bears leaves. What's interesting about the fig tree is that normally it bears its fruit before or at the same time it bears leaves. So when Jesus saw the tree bearing leaves in the distance, He seized the opportunity to teach us a lesson. Jesus was God in the flesh, and God is omniscient—He knows everything about everything. So surely Jesus knew that the tree didn't have fruit on it. So why would He stop by the tree even though He knew He wouldn't be fed from it? He stopped to teach us this lesson.

Symbolically, there are times that we are like that tree. We're in between a place of lack and a place of substance and wholeness and we're not bearing any fruit. Just like the tree was located between two extreme places, its display and lack thereof was in between two extremes. There was no fruit on the tree, but there were leaves. And for a fig tree, leaves are an indicator that there should be fruit. Now here's the key. You may be planted (stuck even!) between a place of lack and abundance, but Jesus is passing by, and He wants to eat of your fruit!

Did it ever occur to you that God wants some of what you've got? It's humbling and frightening to think that God is passing by looking for the fruit that is supposed to be growing on your tree. After all, we've got all of the outward signs that say we should be bearing fruit. We know plenty of scriptures, we wear the appropriate clothes, and we go to church every week. We've got all of the pretty leaves a sanctified tree should ever want.

What is it with these fig tree cover-ups anyway? First Adam, and now us! We don't hold up our end of the bargain, and then when God comes looking for us during the appointed time and season, all we've got to show Him are pretty leaves, as if that will take the place of accomplishing the assignments He's given us. I'm so thankful that God is a patient God. He has to tolerate so much from us. He works with us and pulls at us, and then gives us worth by placing the seed of our purpose within us. He's patient—but He's also looking for us to produce fruit!

So why don't we have any fruit to show for the pretty leaves that we have? Obviously, we have been connected to the water in some way, because we were able to grow leaves. Why weren't we able to finish the fruit-bearing process? Sometimes the answer is that we're content to just show off our leaves, because leaves are signs that we have arrived! We're content to look prosperous and pretty, even if we don't display what God is really after.

Notice, Jesus didn't say, "Oh, well, at least it has leaves. We'll just take the leaves with us on our journey." Jesus was angry enough to curse the thing He had blessed at the beginning of time! God told the trees and plants in Genesis 1 to bring forth fruit based upon the seed that He placed in them. That should tell us something. For Him to change His directive and say "you will *never, ever* grow fruit again" is a strong statement.

Now also notice, Jesus didn't tell the tree to die, He just said that no fruit would grow from it. But in response to His words, the tree withered away! Why? Because once you have no purpose, death is imminent. If you've lost your purpose, you're a dead man walking! Jesus wants to take you with Him to a place where there is peace and wholeness. He doesn't want to take your whole tree, because the flesh and the showy leaves of your tree aren't needed where you're going.

The saying rings true here: only what we do for Christ will last. Only the spiritual things are eternal and worth taking into our land of abundance. God isn't interested in dragging the works of our decaying flesh into our destiny. He wants our flesh to become subject to His Word and commandment over our lives so we can bear fruit. It's our fruit that will bring us into our destiny.

Your fruit, brought to bear by the spiritual seed of God's breath and His Word, has to come forward in order for you to make it into the land of peace. After all, your spirit is the part of you that's living anyway. When you die, you won't take your body, and God wants you to know that while you live, it's not your body that He's interested in taking with Him to your promised land. Your body is only needed because it carries the fruit that will spring forth from the inside of you.

The Lord is passing by each of our trees, and like the parable of the householder who passed by the vineyard each harvest looking for the fruit that wasn't there, He's given us another chance. There are intercessors praying for you and me, asking the Lord to give us another chance, and maybe next season, we'll bear the fruit that we're supposed to bear. As Jesus passes by again, wanting to harvest our fruit, but seeing nothing, our mothers, fathers, pastors, and brothers have interceded asking the Lord to give us another chance (Luke 13:6-9).

But the truth is, all of our chances are running out, and God says we're approaching the final seasons of fruit-bearing opportunities. He's hungry to take us with Him from situations of lack into situations of promise.

But in order to go into this next season, there are some issues we have to leave behind. We can't be concerned about appearance, and just bear leaves so that we can look like all is well. We've got to commit to God's word and commands, unlike the sons in the parable of Matthew 21:28–31. Neither did what their father asked them to do, though one did change his mind and follow instructions. We have to heed God's word for our lives. And finally, we can't be like the glory-seeking people who worked in the vineyard in verses 33–43.

They didn't want to give the householder the fruit that belonged to him in the first place! Their greed ended in murder. They killed the householder's messengers and ultimately killed his son. Sounds familiar, doesn't it? This is what the religious officials did to Jesus, and we do it on a symbolic level as well. We don't receive the warnings or heed the requests that God sends us through His people. Ultimately, we end up stifling and killing our opportunities for Jesus to help us bear fruit in our lives.

"You should have died in the sowing stage! Why get to the reaping stage and faint now?" –Bishop T. D. Jakes

In order to enter into our season of plenty, we can't take these attitudes and issues with us. Just like the vineyard in this last parable, our lives and the fruit that comes from our lives belong to God anyway! It's not ours to be possessive over. And we should consider it a privilege to work in His vineyard. Simply put, stop tripping and get to work!

Get out of the flesh and stop showing off useless leaves. Get into His house and His vineyard and start working! And when He comes to get His fruit and His glory, give them both to Him! He's going to get it one way or another.

We can't afford to take counterproductive habits with us into this next season. We'll only end up stuck, cursed, and withered, in between our history and our destiny. We didn't come this far or work this hard just to stop in the middle of the journey to greatness! It has cost us too much just to try and pull a fast one on God! We are more than conquerors and we're worth much more than an inviting façade, with nothing more to offer than great looks. If Jesus desires something from us, we must have it to give! Give Him what He wants! We can be fruitful and multiply—it's the only way to leave the land of lack and travel to the land of peace.

"How much are you really willing to pay to have what God wants you to have? How much of God do you really want? That's the question. Because then, no price becomes too high, no sacrifice becomes too great if, at the end, you're closer to God."

Co-Pastor Susie C. Owens

TRIAL & ERROR: THE COLOSSIANS TEACH US CHRIST-CENTERED SPIRITUAL SELF ESTEEM

"So there's purpose inside of me. Got it. I've got to work hand-in-hand with God to see that purpose come into fruition. Got that too. But how do I become the best player I can be on this so-called 'team' of Jesus and me? I mean, what does it take to stay on His good side? He's got a lot of running ahead of Him, if He and I are running this relay race together. He's got His part, plus my part, and I've never really been good at these kinds of things. What if I mess up, what if I trip and fall with the baton in my hand, what if I finish last, what if. . ."

Hey! Stop playing the "What-if-I'm-not-good-enough" game. You never win. Take a few lessons from the Colossians. Then pass it on. You and someone you love will be glad you did.

Eating from Your Own Fruit

Colossians 1:3–12

IT IS SO EASY TO GET SIDETRACKED. Maintaining focus is a skill that takes development, a conscientious mindset, and continual discipline. As spiritual beings having an earthly experience, we can get distracted and begin to focus our attention on details, people, and pursuits that don't even matter. They don't guarantee success; they actually distort what success really is, and they divert us from our pursuit of it. Distractions can cause a well-meaning individual to develop wrong practices, motives, and priorities, just like the Colossians in the Bible.

The church at Colosse was a distracted, sidetracked church. When Paul opens his letter to the Colossians, he praises them because he was delighted to hear of their love for God and His people. They had faith in Christ, and Paul thanked God for their conversion to Christianity.

After reading the book of Colossians, though, you'll find out that Paul wasn't happy about everything that took place in the Colossian church: the gospel had been diluted, and somewhere along the way the Colossians developed some false notions about Jesus, His deity, and His absolute Lordship. They had become so misguided, that they had begun to worship angels because they equated the celestial beings with Jesus.

Yes, I know this sounds awful to today's spirit-filled, fire-baptized believer, but it happened. And believe it or not, it happens in today's church, but in more subtle ways.

The Colossians loved Jesus, but they made a wrong turn along their journey on Salvation Boulevard. They lessened their definition and reverence for the Lord Jesus and minimized the image they had of Him when they first met Him.

The Colossians failed to eat from their own fruit.

Paul begins his letter by telling the Colossians that he thanked God for them and that he had permanently placed them on his prayer list. They had received Jesus by faith and had shown love to each other. Paul says that they did so based on the hope they received when they first heard the gospel.

There's just something about the Good News. Do you remember how you felt when you discovered that you had eternal life awaiting you because you received God by faith? You found out that Jesus had a place for you in heaven, even though you didn't (and still don't) deserve it. You had received the precious gift of salvation and, as the old saints used to say, you were "happy-glad"! That's just how the Colossians were—they were so glad to be saved, the world was new, God's people looked better than they ever did, and life was grand.

But apparently, that's where the advancement of their Christian experience halted, because Paul's prayer for them shifts gears. When Paul describes their conversion, he details how the Word of God saved them. They heard the gospel and because faith comes by hearing the Word of God, their faith was stirred and they came to know the grace of God.

They heard the Word, and the Word brought forth fruit in their lives. They knew of the grace of God that would admit them into the pearly gates, but their knowledge stopped there. That's when Paul begins to pray that God would fill them with the knowledge of His will through all spiritual understanding. They had gotten their reservation in heaven, and they really were grateful. They wanted to be more like Christ. Later in

Colossians, we see how they had received faulty teachings about how to achieve true spiritual maturity and fullness in Christ.

They wanted the fruit of Christ, but they were trying to earn it. Now they found themselves erroneously indoctrinated, and Paul had to spend the remainder of his letter straightening them out.

While the rest of this letter helps reconstruct their theology, I believe the solution to preventing this type of breakdown is shared in the opening of the letter in verses 5 and 6. Paul tells them that the gospel they heard produced fruit in them once they gained understanding about God. Then in verse 10, Paul tells them that he's praying for them to receive more knowledge and understanding, so that they can please God and bear fruit in every way.

Well, I thought they had already begun to bear fruit! Why is Paul praying that they restart the process of gaining knowledge and bearing fruit? Because they didn't eat from the first fruit they gained when they received the Lord. There's that fruit, more fruit, and much fruit principle again!

Paul spends the rest of his letter relaying fundamental spiritual foundations because the Colossians needed to go back to the basics. They needed to receive understanding about the gospel, and then they would bear fruit again. From that fruit, they would grow in the knowledge of the Lord.

In short, the more you eat, the more you grow. When you became a Christian, you immediately began to produce fruit. What happened to your fruit? Did it wither and die on the vine? Did you become complacent in your relationship with God? Did worldly principles and ways of living distract you?

The Bible tells us that everything produces fruit after its kind. So if knowledge produced fruit when you first got saved, I encourage you to take a bite of the very fruit you produced. If knowledge caused you to be a fruit-bearing believer, then knowledge will help you continue to bear fruit. You'll be strengthened and you'll be blessed.

The psalmist says it simply:

Don't be satisfied with the first levels of bearing fruit! To consistently bear fruit, we must remain planted by the waters that enabled us to bear our first fruit. We cannot afford to be distracted. Remember what first brought you into

"Blessed is the man who does not walk in the counsel of the wicked or stand in the way of sinners or sit in the seat of mockers. But his delight is in the law of the LORD, and on his law he meditates day and night. He is like a tree planted by streams of water, which yields its fruit in season and whose leaf does not wither. Whatever he does prospers." –Psalm 1:1-3

the kingdom: God's love and grace. And remember what first allowed you to bear fruit: knowledge of who God is in your life. Don't forget, we can never earn the blessings of God—from salvation to prosperity to healing. We'll never be good enough. We'll only become distracted, spending valuable energy on useless pursuits of idol worship.

If you want to produce fruit, eat of the knowledge that brought you your first fruit. Knowledge gives birth to knowledge. If you don't want your leaf to wither, eat of the same knowledge that saved you. Meditate, study, learn the Word of God, and you will, without question, be filled with the knowledge that saves you and shows you the Lord's will for your life, and strengthens you for your Christian walk.

Gaining that knowledge shows us that it was only God's undying love for us that allowed us to come this far. So begin by loving Him and His Word, and don't put undue pressure upon yourself. You can't earn the blessing that God is about to pour out on you. You can only love Him, obey Him, and walk with Him. When you rekindle the love relationship you had with Him when you first met Him, you'll undoubtedly learn more about Him than you ever will from mere hearsay.

So, go ahead, you want to be fruitful don't you? Eat of your own good fruit. It'll help you stay on the right track—and you *will* prosper.

Citizens of the Kingdom

◄◎ *Colossians 1:12–13* ◎►

PREVIOUSLY, WE LEARNED about the church at Colosse. We discovered that they fell into some false teachings that caused them to stop bearing fruit. Fruit is produced when two different entities with compatible qualities have an intimate exchange, cross-pollinating to create offspring. Anytime fruit stops flourishing, you can bet that intimacy is at a low level. That was the case with the Colossians. They found the Lord through the preached Word. They were so excited to be saved, but they didn't pursue their continuing education in the Word of God, and they stopped bearing fruit.

Their lack of intimacy with the Lord and His Word allowed them to receive false teaching. They felt good about being saved. I believe that after they got saved, all of the joy that they had decreased when they found out that they were still imperfect people. I personally know how it feels to be frustrated, because my new walk didn't fully line up with my new talk. We all have areas in our lives that need ongoing regeneration and reconstruction. This regeneration is a process that takes months for some areas, years for others and, ultimately, our entire life is spent in the process of becoming like Jesus.

In Philippians 3, Paul tells us that even he hadn't attained perfection, but he hadn't given up hope either. It can certainly be discouraging for new believers to keep making old mistakes when they've been told that they're a new man or woman.

Apparently, the Colossians struggled in this area. They longed to maintain their "brand-spanking-new" feeling of salvation and discovered that they were still fallible people, capable of sinful words, thoughts, and deeds. Just like when someone buys a new car, the Colossians wanted to keep that "new convert" smell. So guess what they did? They made up their own rules about how to live, what to eat, and when to do what. And they didn't do it by themselves either; they adopted some of the old ordinances that the lawmakers had constructed. These rules gave them a false sense of sanctification, and they felt better about the fact that they couldn't truly obey God's commands in their own strength. Since they couldn't abide by God's laws, they made some laws that they *could* abide by.

In chapter two, we find out that the Colossians had formed a whole set of guidelines so that they would appear to be pleasing to God. They didn't even realize that they were really only trying to please each other with fleshly rules and regulations. Paul asks them a significant question in verses 20–21. If the Colossians were supposed to be dead to the world because of their new life in Christ, why were they aiming so hard to abide by worldly rules?

The truth is that the Colossians were new in the faith and they hadn't learned some important principles. They didn't know how to walk in the Spirit rather than in the flesh. I don't just mean that if they learned to walk in the Spirit they would learn not to sin. Walking in the Spirit is deeper than that. It involves learning that man's measure of what success and wholeness are doesn't matter.

The Colossians had become so concerned about outward appearances and keeping man's rules, they had disregarded their spiritual walk. Walking by faith and not by sight involves more than believing God for a house or a healing; it also means that we can't be encumbered by man's rules, man's opinions, or man's objections. We can't act on or think about man's ideas, especially man's ideas about who each of us is as a person.

Now, this mode of thinking doesn't give us creative license to form rules that allow us to live without restraint. We have to subscribe to our faith and our God for answers about how to live, think, and believe.

The church at Colosse had become so disillusioned, distracted, and preoccupied with men-pleasing rules and regulations that they allowed their faith and their knowledge of God to slip into the background of their consciousness, while carnal rules and regulations took a front seat in their efforts to soothe their consciences.

Anytime we attempt to please men more than God, our flesh stages a takeover! Because men are made in part of flesh, and the flesh is contrary to the Spirit of God within us (Galatians 5:17), the flesh is given power to please itself in every way possible. Our spirits are stifled, and God's love no longer governs our decisions.

This is what happened at the church at Colosse. They were so caught up in fleshly ordinances that other works of the flesh began to run rampant in their community. They had pleased their flesh so much that their flesh began to rule them in areas of sexual immorality, wickedness, and idolatry. They didn't even have good attitudes anymore! Paul had to tell them to stop being angry, unforgiving, and filthy-talking people.

This is an important lesson: when we begin to let the flesh govern our thoughts, words, and actions, it will eventually have total authority over us. The flesh will be king.

It was a flesh parade in mid-winter at Colosse, and the people got sick, so Paul had to take on the role of a spiritual orderly. You know about orderlies that work in the hospital, right? My grandfather called it a "horse-pital," but whatever you call it, Paul's role as an orderly was comparable to that of an actual orderly. He had to wash off God's people with His cleansing Word, and he had to change their bedpans. You get my point—there was a whole lot of mess up in there! Paul had a whole lot to deal with, so he took the Colossians back to the basics.

One of the first foundational principles that Paul had to teach the Colossians is that they had been delivered from the power of darkness and brought into the kingdom. The people needed this reminder because they had forgotten, or didn't fully understand, that they were citizens in a new kingdom—the kingdom of God.

They had been struggling to maintain their status in man's kingdom by continually paying dues with their flesh, and they couldn't effectively take their position in God's kingdom. Even today, sometimes we miss some of the benefits of being in the kingdom. There are three important aspects of citizenship in the kingdom of God.

The Bible tells us that the kingdom of God is not about physical things like eating and drinking, but it's righteousness, peace, and joy in the Holy Spirit (Romans 14:17). It was so important for the Colossians to know that in this kingdom, they already had righteousness, or right standing with God. Fully understanding this would stop their desire to create rules and guidelines just to try to appear righteous. They would have understood that people couldn't make them abide by ineffective laws and traditions. They would have known that the kingdom in which they were citizens gave them righteousness, even when they messed up. Righteousness is a gift. The Bible says that Abraham believed God and it was accounted to him as righteousness (Galatians 3:6).

It is our faith and belief in God that grants us righteousness. The Colossians needed to know that they didn't have to earn it—they already had it! They had received by God's grace, and their faith in Christ gave them the gift of righteousness. It can't be earned; it's given to every believer.

> *We don't want to live sinful lives as if we've never received salvation, but when we do mess up, we have to know who we are, whose we are, and where we live.* ☙

This aspect of God's kingdom is so important because it delivers us from trying to please people, it looses us from the chains of tradition that give us a false sense of righteousness and holiness, and it frees us from the frustration of feeling imperfect, inadequate, and unusable. We will make mistakes in one way or another as long as we're living on this earth. But we have to know that we are citizens in right standing in the kingdom of God.

No, we don't want to live sinful lives as if we've never received salvation, but when we do mess up, we have to know who we are, whose we are, and where we live.

We don't have to try and please people, or ascribe to our own definition of holiness. We don't have to participate in rituals and routines just so we can feel better about our hidden imperfections. We can't do this because, like the Colossians, we'll become so entangled with trying to fit man's description of a Christian, we'll end up in more sin than before.

I've got to keep reminding myself that I have righteousness because I'm a part of God's kingdom. What freedom and liberty I have, knowing that despite faults, weaknesses, and all, my faith in God gives me righteousness! And because I have right standing *with* God, I have access *to* God. He looks at me and sees His grace and love and allows me to have an open relationship with Him.

And righteousness doesn't just encompass feeling cleansed from sin. But being in right standing with God means knowing that I am in the right position to receive the blessings—and even the insight of God! I'm in the right position to be creative on my job and my ministry because now I've got access to the mind and creativity of God Himself! I live in the right land to be free from sickness, poverty, and depression! I *am* the righteousness of God!

And with that righteousness comes peace. Peace helps me cope with life's unfair circumstances. Peace brings wholeness to fragmented, fractured situations.

Though everything isn't perfect, and life's storm is raging, peace allows us to say, "It is well." I'm glad that peace comes in this kingdom package. Everything won't be perfect at the same time, but peace fills in the gaps, mends the tears, and connects the disconnections that are in our lives. Peace doesn't always solve the problem, but it always allows us to travel through the storm. Because we are citizens of the kingdom of God, we have peace with God, with ourselves, and with life's "unpeaceful" circumstances.

Along with righteousness and peace, we have joy as believers. We have joy because we live where God lives, in His kingdom—and where God reigns is where His presence lives. And the Bible says that in His presence, there is fullness of joy. When we make being in His presence a daily part of our lives, we'll have joy that helps us overcome any sadness, any heartache, and any pain.

Just being in the kingdom is reason enough to have joy! I don't have to fight life's battles alone; I've gained victory over the power of darkness, and I have a right to joy! I have a right to peace and I have a right to have access to God—He brought me in, just as I was. He saved me and my intimate relationship with Him has caused me to bear fruit in His kingdom. Man's laws do not bind me because I'm in the kingdom, and being in the kingdom has empowered me to bear fruit and to live a life filled with purpose.

I don't ever have to overcompensate for any imperfections in my life. I can be fruitful and I am destined to multiply, because I am a citizen of the kingdom!

How to Avoid Brain Damage

Colossians 2:10, 18; Psalm 95:6

PAUL REALLY LOVED THE COLOSSIANS. He prayed for them, he took time to encourage them, and he took time to set them straight! They were on a very destructive path. They had received false teaching and it had started a fire fueled by pagan philosophies, blasphemous beliefs, and corrupt customs. They were in trouble alright.

Anytime you see Paul having to explain why Jesus is Lord, you must know that the enemy is at work somewhere. The Bible tells us that no man can say that Jesus is Lord except by the power of the Holy Spirit. Consequently, any man, woman, or entity that tries to convince us otherwise operates by a power that is absolutely not from the Holy Spirit.

The Colossians were deceived. They had started to believe that they needed to participate in observances of holidays and other traditions just to prove they were saved. At first glance, it doesn't sound so bad that they wore certain clothes and celebrated certain holidays. What's so wrong about eating certain foods? To the average person, these acts almost sound commendable. Here are people who are highly disciplined, right? Wrong!

The Colossians believed participating in these fruitless acts would help maintain their right-standing relationship with God. This is the problem: if you feel that you have to work and earn the salvation and righteousness that are supposed to be gifts from God, you have decided that the blood and the name of Jesus aren't powerful enough to deem you saved and righteous by themselves. That means Jesus could not be all that He's cracked up to be, and everything that He promised you may not be true.

That's the kind of mentality the Colossians had assumed. They were misguided, and unfortunately, they had even started worshiping angels, because they were divine beings just like Jesus. It almost seems as though they figured that they should cover their bases, and worship any unseen thing that may have some power.

Jesus is the ONLY One who is worthy of our worship. ☺

Imagine how detrimental this kind of thinking can be! There are some unseen entities that should not have our worship. Jesus is the ONLY One who is worthy of our worship. That's why Paul took so much time in the first two chapters of Colossians to tell us just how entirely and absolutely Jesus is Lord. In chapter one, he explains how Jesus was not just a divine man, but how He is also the complete image of God, who came to earth in the flesh to save us from our sins. He was God in the flesh, and no less! He didn't come to earth to do good works; He *was* the good work in action. He created all things, and by Him all things consist (1:17). That means that before anything ever was, angels or otherwise, He existed, and anything that is was created by Him and exists because of Him.

It seems so silly for us today to think about worshiping angels, but if we're not careful, we can operate under the same misconceptions that the Colossians did.

The problem was that the Colossians failed to acknowledge Jesus' deity. That was obvious when they started worshiping the things He made more than they worshiped Him. Who was more brilliant, the light bulb or Thomas Edison? Well, duh! The light bulb only does what Edison designed it to do. Without him, there would be no light bulb. So why esteem the light bulb higher than its inventor?

But we often do the same thing. God made angels. Psalms says that He assigns angels to surround us and protect us from evil. It wouldn't make sense to start thanking and worshiping the angels for protecting us, because it's really God who protects us through the angels He created.

So many times, we worship the blessings that God gave us, rather than worshiping Him. We may not bow down and say, "Husband, wife, Mom, Dad, house, car, job, friends, I worship and adore you..." but our actions do. We give more deference to them than we do the things of God. We consider spending time with the Lord, whether at church or just one-on-one, to be drudgery, but we have no problem rearranging our entire schedules to accommodate a person. We've even been guilty of disobeying God just to win the approval of man.

I think that in one way or another, we've all been a perpetrator of this crime. We've worshiped the creation more than the Creator of the creation. The Bible says that our God is jealous, and He doesn't want anyone to take His place. As a matter of fact, that's one of the quickest ways to incite God's wrath and make His jealousy flair up.

All parents have that one thing that sets them off. If you have kids, you know what I mean. If you don't, then you may remember when you would do that one thing that would drive your parents crazy. Well, this just may be God's one thing. And if you set Him off, He'll do just like Mama and Daddy did—He'll snatch you!

Paul was concerned for the Colossians. They were new converts and were about to get snatched! In Colossians 2:18, he tells them not to succumb to teachings that will cause them to do crazy things like worship angels.

Here's what really catches my attention. Paul says anyone who condemns you for worshiping God instead of idols is like a person whose body has lost connection with his head. Well, anytime a person's body has lost connection with the head, the doctors declare him brain-dead! That means that the head can't control the body, the body can't function, and it certainly can't grow.

That's just what has happened to some of us. Somehow, we've gotten out of order and begun to serve the wrong master. And we've done it all while flailing our arms and hollering at the top of our lungs, "Bless me! Bless me, Lord!"

Do you know that you won't advance into the next level of blessings predestined for your life until your worship comes into proper, God-ordained, spiritual order? That may be why relationships with friends and loved ones are being challenged. The Lord may not allow you to be married, because He knows you'll deify (make god) your spouse, and God ain't havin' it!

Paul told the Colossians in verse 19 that if they participated in this behavior, they would be brain-dead and would not grow, as God would have them grow.

Have you noticed some stifled, stunted areas in your life? Have you advanced in some areas and been severely retarded in others? Have you allowed childhood hurts to cause you to pursue certain positions, relationships, and recognition, as if when you achieved them, you would have attained perfection?

Well, those things have become your god, and God is jealous! Have you noticed that each time you grab hold to that one thing you've been trying so hard to achieve, it somehow slips away, or you get it but you're still unfulfilled? When you do achieve it, your excitement quickly wanes and you don't feel any better than before, because you're still disconnected from God in some area.

You're trying to fill a void with something God wants to give you, rather than filling that void with God. You just may be brain-dead, and you'll never grow, heal, flourish, or bear fruit in that area until you get your priorities in order. We can't bear fruit if we're not attached to God, who is our True Vine.

God wants to bless you with prosperity, healthy relationships, and exciting endeavors, but He won't do it if He has to keep snatching you, and snatching them from you.

So go ahead, be fruitful by staying connected to the True Vine. Worship your Maker, and He'll give you everything that He's made for you because He can trust you. He won't have to snatch you, because you're not brain-dead! You're connected to the Lord in prayer, praise, and worship, and you're fully functional, growing in knowledge and in grace in every area of your life!

Pass It On!

◈ *Colossians 4:3, 16* ◈

PAUL HAD DONE HIS BEST to straighten the Colossians out, and it was time to close his letter. As he hastens to give his final thoughts on service and submission, Paul begins his descent on what has been an eventful journey of much-needed spiritual correction. After a turbulent, yet comfortable ride on the aircraft, he unbuckles his safety belt and prepares to deplane from his flight on Apostolic Airways. He strolls down the aisle of the immaculately clean stark-white cabin, giving his final shoutouts and high-fives to those who were aboard this fantastic flight with him.

He tells some of them, "Holla at me later! Ari [also known as Aristarchus] and Marcus told me to tell you 'what's up!' And if I send Marcus back here to help y'all, don't act a fool, now!"

He tells others, "Tell Archie (or Archipus) I said it's time for him to come up here with the big boys and stop coppin' out! Holla back!"

That's how I normally read the end of Paul's letters. It's a whole bunch of names and a whole bunch of hellos, right? It was really addressed directly to the recipient of the letter and has nothing to do with me, right? Well, that's what I thought until the Holy Spirit kindly showed me the essence of what transpired during Paul's closing of this particular letter.

What would I do with the Holy Spirit? I'd read the Bible, enjoy some of it, but miss much of the most vital information because my human mind would disregard it, being subject to carnal logic and immature reasoning. The Lord is wonderful, isn't He? He brings light to the spiritual things that are hidden from our natural view.

Amid what seems to be a long directory of the most commonly mispronounced Greek names are some notes on apostolic order, examples of true fellowship between churches, and a depiction of the heart of a true apostle. We miss it because the names are long, and we don't really believe that the last part of the letter relates to us.

But they do. Paul says a couple of interesting things in verses 3 and 16 of the final chapter of Colossians. Many people who frequent the church have heard some form of the phrase, "Paul, a prisoner of the gospel..." We've heard it so much, that we almost disregard its real meaning. We automatically recall how Paul was imprisoned with Silas and others, and how he was beat up. I believe we have almost become desensitized to the real sacrifice that the first apostles offered to God and to the church, as they labored to help define it. It was a significant sacrifice. It may seem prehistoric and outdated, but you'll see its magnitude if you put yourself in Paul, Peter, or John's place.

Are you willing to be jailed, crucified upside down, or brutally decapitated to spread the gospel? Truthfully, many of us can't fathom the suffering the early saints incurred. When we think prison, we think county jail. When we think crucifixion, we think being stapled to a 2x4 and sipping some vinegar. We don't really get it. It was much more than that. With careful study, we find that Paul often had to defecate on himself while residing for months in a room not much bigger than a porta-potty. So when Paul says that he's in bonds for the gospel, we have to understand just what he means.

In 4:13, he asks the Colossians to pray that the Lord give him another opportunity to speak the Word of God to anyone willing to listen. Spreading the gospel was all Paul had. It wasn't the prestigious career that people associate with today's popular clergy. It was hard work then, and it's hard work now. Now, Paul was a learned man. At any time, couldn't he just cancel all of his revivals and crusades? Why didn't he just snap his pencil in half and stop writing letters? Couldn't he have easily taken up another career? He spoke several languages, was a tentmaker, and had clout with the Jewish high priest before his conversion. He obviously had a variety of skills and great leadership ability, so why did he "settle" for being a prisoner of the gospel?

Well, Paul was more than just a prisoner in the physical sense. When he wrote of being a prisoner, I really believe he was referring more to the spiritual indebtedness that he had since his conversion. He was indebted and obligated to preach the Word. He encountered physical jail cells to do so, but I believe he would have been as much a prisoner if he had never darkened the doors of any prison.

Paul was indebted to the Lord and to the Word because he found out just how much the gospel was able to change lives. He learned it first-hand. Don't forget, Paul was more than a very mean persecutor of believers. He was a murderer. A first-rate, cutthroat killer! He took pride in giving Christians a hard time—until he had an eye-opening encounter with the Lord.

Paul (then named Saul) was stricken with blindness, just so he could receive spiritual sight. He went from killer to healer in days. He changed from bigoted to big-hearted in months. He went from persecutor to prisoner in a few short years. What he used to be, he no longer was, and he had genuinely experienced the changing power of the blood and the name of Jesus.

So, he gladly put on chains and fetters to deliver the saving and healing Word of God to the Gentiles he once hated. He thrived off of teaching about the grace of God. He lived to tell sinners how they could be reconciled to God. And he died telling the saints how to live fruitful lives.

As he closed his letters, he often left final words and instructions. The letter to the church at Colosse was no different. Take a moment and look past the names and places and discover what Paul wants us, the modern-day believers, to do.

According to verse 16, he wants us to pass on the message. That's all. Paul had been changed, and he made efforts to tell anyone who reads his letters that they can change too. He was a murderer.

Someone reading this book may have killed someone. Someone else is secretly skimming the lines of this book and remembering the time they stole thousands of dollars in property or merchandise. Still someone else is turning these pages, vividly recalling the magnitude of their numerous sexual exploits.

Some people act as though they've forgotten their past. But Paul never told us to forget what the Lord has done for us. Sometimes we act as though we've been living holy lives since we were old enough to utter the word *sacred*. But Paul wants us to tell our stories. Now don't tell it all!

Some of us were liars, cheaters, and thieves. But the blood of the Lamb has washed us. Jesus has changed our lives. If you really know you have been changed and that the angels in heaven have signed your name, don't wait until you cross the Jordan to tell it! Pass it on!

Someone is desperate to hear your story, to know that it is possible to truly change and live for Jesus. Yes, we're all in the process of becoming totally whole, but if God has done *anything* for you—you ought to tell it. Tell it until people begin to encounter the saving power of Jesus for themselves! Tell it until you shame the enemy and his allies! And yes, tell it until you remind yourself just how far you've come and how much God has shown His Love to you! He's been so good, so loving, and oh, so merciful!

And if He's done wonderful things for you before, He's sure to do more! Things may not be perfect now, but the memory of what God has done in the past is just a reminder that there are still better days ahead! Be like David and encourage yourself in the Lord (1 Samuel 30:6). Don't hold back; put yourself in remembrance of how good God is.

So go ahead, tell how the Lord has blessed you, how He's brought fruit into your life, and take time to be strengthened as someone else shares their story with you. Even then, you'll find that you're bearing fruit. When you tell others about the goodness of God, that is praise.

As a matter of fact, this is the basis of praise. Praise is a celebration of God. It takes place between people. One tells of the goodness and character of God, and another replies with details of his perception of God's divine qualities. And the sacrifice of praise is the fruit of our lips. Anytime you part your lips to tell the story of all that God has brought you through, you give Him glory, which is a sacrifice of praise, and fruit will follow!

Fruit will follow and healing will follow, as well, when you tell your story. The more you tell your story, the more you put your past behind you while putting God's grace in front of you, and the more you'll be able to walk into the stages of bearing fruit, more fruit, and much fruit.

There is no monopoly on God's goodness, or on the things He's taught you and blessed you with. So, PASS IT ON! ⋙

The bottom line: there is no monopoly on God's goodness, or on the things He's taught you and blessed you with. So, PASS IT ON! The more you give to others, even if it's just a testimony of God's goodness, the more you participate in the process of receiving His blessings.

As you give power to others by teaching them about God's power and grace, the more you'll be empowered. Each time you give, you remind yourself that you're not a victim, but you're blessed enough to give and to share what God has done for you.

Remember, we overcome by the blood of the Lamb and the word of our testimony. The two join together and create the sound of victory that resounds into eternity, releasing blessings upon all who hear it. So don't just sit there. PASS IT ON!

"Every time I would go back and hold a hurting little broken girl,
I was holding myself."

Paula White

Part 2

More Fruit

Confronting Temptation and Inner Conflict

"We're on the move, and we're bearing fruit! And it's better than I imagined! I feel a sense of purpose and fulfillment. Life is grand and I'm on my way... Hold on! What's that sound? Hey, wait a minute. That looks like a chainsaw! What do you mean it's for my own good? Well it sure does hurt! I'm not sure I like this fruit thing anymore!"

Pruning time is never easy, especially when you've got to face some hard facts about yourself. Did I mention this might be a bumpy ride? Well, hold on to your hats, because here we go...

Provision for the Vision

✦ *Genesis 1:20–25; Genesis 3* ✦

BEFORE GOD EVER FORMED MAN from the dust of the ground, He made a place for man to live. And it wasn't just a place to live; it was an environment for which man could perform the tasks God had assigned him.

In Genesis 1:20–22, it's important to note that the environment that needed Adam's care was prepared for him before he ever arrived on the scene. When God gives you a vision and instruction, it's critical to keep in mind that He's given you an assignment, not because you need to have something to do, but because there's a need for what you have to offer the world around you.

God made the fish, the birds, and animals before He made man. But they all needed man to thrive. Then, God placed the mandate on man to care for nature, and put inside man the gift and the ability needed for the task. God is deliberate in everything He does. He didn't allow man to *try* and name the animals. God gave man the ability to do so before He ever told the man to name them. God desires for mankind, and believers in particular, to be successful and affect the atmosphere around them.

I've come to realize that there are places where the Lord sent me to be a help and a blessing to the environment around me. Looking at this scriptural example, I know that the part I would play was made specifically for me,

51

before I ever arrived. Whether I was a solution to a problem, filler of a void, or the missing piece to a puzzle, I've learned that God has so many particular purposes for us when He sends us to places, to jobs, and into the lives of others.

Now many of us may have heard this before. But sometimes, it's worth being reminded that there is a reason for everything. Not only that, we must also know that if God has sent us into a situation to be a blessing, He's placed whatever we need inside and outside of us to thrive in that environment.

On the inside, Adam had the capacity and ability to administrate the affairs of the earth. God had provided him with the necessary gifts and talents.

On the outside, the Lord provided Adam with substance with which he could eat, drink, and live while he performed the task that God had commissioned.

We must understand that if God has commissioned us to perform a work for His kingdom, we have what it takes inside and outside of us to complete the work. With every dream and vision, there is certainly a provision. There's a provision to perform and succeed at the task, and there's a provision to survive and thrive in the process.

Although this is a message that we've heard many times, I believe there are a few more principles to learn from this story as we strive to bear fruit for the kingdom of God.

We must also note that just as it was in the Garden of Eden, there will be a certain element of temptation existent while we do what God has called us to do. And the temptation will generally involve us attempting to step outside of our God-given role and into a realm either above or beneath our privilege.

Adam and Eve sinned against God when they jumped at the chance to seemingly be more like God. They ate of the forbidden fruit at the suggestion of Satan, who was masquerading as a serpent. God had warned them about the fruit of that tree, but when they allowed themselves to be deceived, they ate the fruit anyway, believing they would be more like God.

They didn't realize that disobeying God's Word would never make them any more like Him than they already were. God cannot go against His own Word; He is His Word (John 1) and He cannot work against Himself. He and His Word are in direct agreement. For Adam and Eve to disobey God and His

Word, they only brought themselves out of alignment with God. How then could they be more like Him, if they were separated from Him?

Like Adam and Eve, even when we are placed in the garden of our destiny, complete with God's provision for our lives, we must be aware that somewhere in that garden lies the temptation to reach outside of the realm of authority and action that God has called us to. Simply put, there are some things that God has not called us to do. It may be within our reach, but not within our power to handle, control, or maintain. It's just not meant for us to do.

So we should stay focused, centered, and grounded in the realm of responsibility that God has called us to. No further, and no less. And frankly, what He's intended for us to do is enough.

I, for one, have seen both sides of the coin. I've tried to do more than I was called to—at work, church, and in other people's lives. It can be tricky, because, like Adam and Eve, our intention may be to follow God with all of our hearts and endear ourselves to Him all the more. But that childlike desire to be like our Father can turn into an unhealthy desire to *be* our Father. In the end, all that we create for ourselves is chaos. We simply cannot be more to people, our jobs, or our ministries than God has designed us to be. We certainly can't be more to them than God Himself is to them.

But, we can't be less than He's called us to be to them either. Both scenarios bring much frustration and leave us feeling further from God's will than before.

Many times, just like Adam and Eve, there are times that we stray so far from God's will and touch the untouchable that God has to send us away from what was to be our dwelling. Not only have we ruined and tainted the environment, we've also forfeited our role as keeper of the God-given grounds that He's sent us to, and consequently, God has to banish us from the premises.

I speak symbolically in terms of the fall of man and the subsequent events in Genesis 3, but I'm sure that many of us know the feeling.

I know I do. There have been areas of ministry, school, and relationships that the Lord has blessed me to partake of and be a blessing to, but because I touched the untouchable, God had to banish me—by my participation or even physically. And just as He placed cherubs on the outside of the garden, I know that there are some "places" in my life that I'll never again be able to visit.

I've matured past the place where I say to myself, "Well, it must have never been God's will for me to do this or that, or to meet this person or that person." Or, worse, "God, You put me in this situation, knowing I couldn't handle it! I blame You for this. Why didn't You just let me go on doing what I was doing before?"

As humans do, even as Adam and Eve did, we all have the tendency to live in regret, or to spiritualize the situation, and even point the finger at God, saying, "You should have never let me experience this! I was doing just fine by myself. But, no! You just had to put me to sleep! You just had to take one of my ribs and give me this trifling wife! It's all Your fault, God!"

We can't assume this mentality, or we'll never grow, and we'll most certainly never bear the kind of fruit God wants us to bear. We've got to realize that God wants only good for His children. We've also got to realize that every blessing He gives us has the capability to be harmful. And it's not His fault. God has given man the power of choice. We are free, moral agents.

Here's an example: Many of us know some gifted and talented people, who are, for lack of better terms, thugs, criminals, con artists, and hustlers. They have wonderful minds, keen business sense, sparkling personalities, and the gift of gab. But they use it all for doing wrong.

> *He won't let us encounter tempting circumstances and lying voices without giving us the final word about them.* ❧

And when we look at these people, we shake our head and think, *Wouldn't this person's gift be much better utilized in the kingdom of God?* Let's face it: mob bosses have great leadership skills. And though some of that talent may be cloaked in fear and intimidation, there is a certain amount of talent and even discernment that is required to survive in "that line of work."

Well, we can't blame God because these people are good at what they do! Similarly, we can't blame God for trying to bless us. What we do with our gifts, talents, and opportunities is our choice. And we must not blame God for our stupid decisions, no matter what our original intentions were! The fact of the matter is, just as in the case of Adam and Eve, God has always given us some sort of warning about the temptation to come.

Sometimes we look at that story and think that God made the forbidden fruit more desirable by telling the first man not to eat of it. But a more accurate way to look at this story is that God warned Adam about the tree before the serpent ever came to tempt him!

He won't let us encounter tempting circumstances and lying voices without giving us the final word about them. God is the Final Word! That is the way that Jesus overcame His time of temptation. He gave Satan, His tempter, God's Word—the Final Word—on the situation. And He had to do it more than one time! When God told Adam that they were not to eat of the tree, they had the final word on the situation. But as most of us have done at some point in our lives, they didn't stand on that Word.

Now, we, like Eve, will put up some form of resistance, but eventually we cave in—all because the temptation actually appeals to our senses in one way or another. It sounds, feels, looks, smells, or tastes good, or otherwise boosts our egos in some way.

Until we can get to the point in our lives that the Word of God, written in the Bible or spoken to us in our spirits, is the final word and our first line of defense, we'll continue to cave in to the enemy's devices.

I don't think I'm alone when I say that this is an area of my life that will always be in process. As I arrive at the different gardens and havens that God sends me to, whether they are jobs, ministries, relationships, or other opportunities to bear fruit, I realize that there will always be an element of temptation. But I keep reminding myself that God has already made provision for the vision that He's placed inside of me.

He's given me talents to complete the task, and He's given me extrinsic resources to enjoy while I'm there. He's also given me the Final Word of warning. There *is* an untouchable substance that I must avoid. It's all up to me. If I want God's vision for my life to come to pass, I must rely on my internal gifts, my external resources, and God's Final Word for my situation.

Provision for the Vision, part II

✤ *Genesis 3* ✤

GOD IS SO MERCIFUL AND FAITHFUL that His provision even supercedes our failures. What's so great about the story of Adam and Eve is Genesis 3:21. After their rebellion, God doles out consequences for their actions.

There *are* consequences for our disobedience. And like Adam and Eve (and sometimes more so, in my opinion), our consequences are laced with grace. After giving them punishment for their crime of treason, God takes the time to slay an innocent animal and clothe the couple. Not only is this a sign of the shed blood of the coming Messiah, but it is also a beautiful picture of a loving father longing to comfort his children in a most uncomfortable situation. This act shows God's heart for His children.

He must send them away from the Garden, if nothing else, for their own good. God didn't want Adam and Eve to partake of spiritual death and then eat from the tree of life and have to stay in a perpetual state of spiritual death. So He sent them away and placed angels outside of the Garden to keep watch so that man could never enter there again.

The killing of the animal and God sending Adam and Eve away from the Garden all point to God's provision for the vision that He has for man. Ultimately, God's plan is to have perfect fellowship with His creation. He knew that He couldn't have it if they were caught in a state of death and separation from Him forever, so He sent them away.

He also clothed them, showing His concern for their concerns. In Genesis 3:10, Adam's explanation for hiding from God is that He was naked and ashamed. Remember, God always knew they were naked, so He wasn't bothered by it; it was Adam who was uncomfortable with his nakedness.

It really is true: God is concerned about the issues that concern us.

Some people depict God as an absolutely mean, old guy, far removed from our feelings. But this story shows a contrary representation. Just think, if Adam and Eve couldn't face their Father because they were ashamed of their nakedness, how could they accomplish anything He would assign them to do?

After all, without Him, we can do nothing (John 15:5). So if Adam and Eve had continued to hide from God, they would have never seen their purpose fulfilled, because it takes the unlikely pairing of an absolutely undefeated God and an entirely dependent man to accomplish God's will on the earth! So He chastised them, but He also comforted them, and it was all so His purpose for their lives could be fulfilled.

God is so committed to His plan for our lives that He's willing to jump over the hurdles of issues that bother us, because they don't bother Him! He is the supreme example of a great parent. He's stern and firm when He needs to be, all while showing love, affirmation, and tolerance for our immaturity.

God was concerned with the things that concerned Adam and Eve, just like He is with us. So He clothed the first men, not just to ease their pain, but also to remind us that though we've messed up, He's provided all men with the blood of Jesus. He's clothed us with His own righteousness and given us a reason to live, and even better, to live for Him!

Our reason for living for God is never payback, because God desires more than a master-slave relationship with us. We're His children, and we could never repay Him with the same quality of sacrifice because our redemption is based not just upon perfect, spotless blood, but also upon love.

Shedding our blood, sweat, and tears is not enough, particularly if we fail to see the big picture: God sent His Son to save us because of His *love* for the world, not because He needed to buy our services.

So stop trying to beat God's giving! You can't and you won't, no matter how hard you try! Instead, look at the coat He draped around your shoulders when you were at your lowest point. This coat is not one of pity, but one of love. Remind yourself that Someone had to die so that you could escape whatever mess God graciously sent you away from.

It takes the unlikely pairing of an absolutely undefeated God and an entirely dependent man to accomplish God's will on the earth!

And when you think about these acts of God, recognize that love motivated them. Look at the coat and see it as a covering. The cost of that covering is proof that after all of your mistakes, God, just as He did with Adam and Eve, still desires to see you successfully produce His destiny for your life. None of this was a cold business transaction, but it was, instead, an act of love. God knows that you'll never feel true fulfillment unless you completely actualize the dream that He's placed on the inside of you.

God's Word stands forever (1 Peter 1:25), and every good and perfect gift comes from Him! And there's not even a remote possibility of Him changing (James 1:17). He decided how He would use us before the world was framed, and though we've made mistakes, His goal is to see His purpose fulfilled. His Word and His will are *that* strong.

When we disobey Him, He somehow finds a way to show us His love and grace, not just because He feels sorry for us, but because He is providing a provision for the vision He's planted inside of us.

Through this story, God says to me, "The way you can tell that I still had a plan for Adam and Eve is that I clothed them and gave them a way to escape perpetual death."

And the same is true for us. We've all failed Him, but even in our failure we've been given a way out! We've been given more than a ticket to eternal life too. God sent Adam and Eve away, but they still had an assignment.

This is a message to the fallen believer. Though once in harmonious fellowship with God, the fact that you've made horrible mistakes does not mean that God has canceled His plans for your life. Similar to the tree we discussed in "Don't Take It With You," God gives periods of grace to us. And though He must chasten us as fathers should, He shows His love, making the load of guilt and shame we carry lighter.

And He does so out of compassion and because He still has plans for our lives. God is still longing for His kingdom to benefit from the fruit that He's called us to bear!

So when you serve Him and offer your life as a sacrifice to Him, don't do so based on mere obligation, but return the love that God has shown you! We've all messed up, and messed up bad, but it was God's love that provided correction and comfort so that we could return to our purpose in life.

When God sent Adam and Eve away from the Garden of Eden, He didn't cancel His plans for them or for mankind. Throughout the book of Genesis and the Bible, God continues to instruct man to be fruitful and multiply. Not one of the people He gave this instruction to was infallible. They were all battling sinful flesh. But God parented them, as He desires to parent us, and patiently guided them toward their purpose. And still, He says, "Be fruitful and multiply."

With God's chastening there is always a measure of grace. This mixture of discipline and grace is designed to show us that we are never far from God's love for us. As long as we're on this earth there is still a purpose for our lives, no matter how bad we feel we've messed up.

It happened to Adam and Eve—and remember, the seed of all mankind was inside of them, so it happened to us too—and it's still happening to us today. God chastised them, but they still had work to do—and it was work—but they didn't go without the grace of God. God says that His grace is sufficient (2 Corinthians 12:9) to accomplish any task, even when we encounter challenges in our walk with Him. God's grace and discipline all point to His strong love for us, and they're all provision for His vision for our lives.

Give it UP!

« *Proverbs 18:16* »

WE CAN'T TALK ABOUT BEING FRUITFUL or planting seeds without talking about the ministry of giving. Giving is just that; it's a ministry. Giving of yourself, your time, and your finances is a ministry. Giving to others is a ministry, and it's a ministry to God. People may benefit, but God receives it as if you were giving it straight to Him.

That's what the Bible says about being faithful in your job or in other positions of service, whether you're paid or not. Obedient service "as unto the Christ" means that even when your boss or authority figure is unfair, under qualified, or just plain mean, you are to work as if you answer directly to God (Ephesians 6:5)!

Believe it or not, God honors you when you maintain your composure and work as though He was the only One watching. Really, if no one else is watching you, God is, and that's what's most important.

You see, giving is about so much more than giving money. Many Christians have the tithes and offerings routine down, and that is a teaching that must not be overlooked when discussing giving. Tithing—giving ten percent of your entire financial income—is symbolic of your whole life. It says to God, "All that I have is Yours." Tithing says that not just your paycheck belongs to God, but your life, because the Bible tells us that wherever our treasures (or earthly riches, especially money) are, our hearts will be right there with them (Matthew 6:21).

If you give God your financial ten percent, you're saying that your heart belongs to Him as well. But, as you probably know through life's experiences, it is possible to *say* something and *live* something quite different. I don't know about you, but I have given my tithe, noting that all I have belongs to God, but went to my job and complained about how much I couldn't stand it, and couldn't wait until I got another "gig."

But I didn't need another job; I needed a better attitude. Finally, somewhere along the way, I began to take the scripture seriously that tells us that a man's gift makes room for him and brings him before great men (Proverbs 18:16). And I decided that my gifts, my time, and my talents were much better served if I first gave them all to God and allowed Him to bring me before the people who needed to experience them.

I also decided that I didn't want to be before great men with a raunchy attitude. I actually made a decision not to willfully leave any job with bad feelings. I decided that I didn't want to look back on any season in my life with regret, wondering what I could have done better or what would have happened if I had exhibited a different attitude. Then while I was contemplating my attitude and my own need for improvement, I realized that I had allowed my own personal hang-ups to interfere with my performance.

Did I have an exemplary work reputation with my company and most every employer before or since? Yes, but God was calling me to a higher level of giving. That's right. On a paid job, God called me to a higher level of giving. The Word of God tells us that we are to submit to those in authority with the understanding that we are submitting to God. But how many of us really go to our jobs or to our auxiliaries at church with the mindset that we're clocking in and out of God's payroll system?

Really, that's exactly what we're doing. God is tracking our performance, and most importantly He's monitoring our progress. God's report card is not always about perfection; it's about steadily maturing as you walk toward your destiny.

When you consider the concept of giving, consider this: everything you give—whether it's your time, money, or effort—anytime you give, whether at your church, job, or to your family members, whether you're being compensated financially or not, God is the number one recipient of your giving.

At the point that your giving truly touches the heart of God, you'll begin to be brought before great men. Sometimes we think that we need to be seen giving or going the extra mile at work or at church, but really, as long as God sees you, sooner or later, you'll be brought before people who are great in the eyes of both God and man.

> *God's report card is not always about perfection; it's about steadily maturing as you walk toward your destiny.*

I've experienced this principle personally. When I was a nineteen-year-old college student in Dallas, Texas, I became an intern at what has been cited as one of America's fastest growing churches, The Potter's House. The pastor, Bishop T. D. Jakes was one of the few ministers on television that I hailed as one of my favorite preachers. I guess I have good taste in ministry (along with many other believers), because *Time* magazine named him America's best preacher.

Before I go further, let me backtrack a bit to my senior year in high school. I grew up in Albuquerque, New Mexico, and decided that I wanted to go to an out-of-state college. I had it all planned out. I had evaluated colleges based on high criteria (city, weather, proximity to New Mexico, and, oh yeah, the school's academics) and decided that I wanted to go to Northwestern University in Evanston, Illinois, north of Chicago.

I planned to attend their acclaimed Medill School of Journalism, get an internship on *The Oprah Winfrey Show*, and end up working as a reporter at a news station until finally (about five years after college!), I would work for *Dateline* on NBC. I had it all planned out!

It was winter break, and because I was very involved in extracurricular activities in high school, the holiday vacation gave me an opportunity to sit down and complete some college applications *early* before the start of the spring semester of my final year of high school.

I was almost proud: I was taking the initiative and completing the application materials early, just knowing that by that time next year, I would be a student in cold Illinois, traveling back to New Mexico for the holidays.

Well, I must have slept through the reading of the application materials and neglected to read that the final deadline for application to Northwestern was in December. There were no early-January or mid-February application deadlines. December was it. And I had missed the application deadline by just three days.

Needless to say, I was more than bummed out. I was shocked. I was upset. I was mad at Northwestern's "stupid" early deadline, yet secretly impressed by the prestige that exuded from the statement it made. Northwestern didn't have time to wait for the "regular" high school applicants to turn in their forms at the last minute. Such a prestigious school wasn't hard up for enrollees. And here I was, slacker numero uno, missing the deadline by three days. I was disappointed in myself, and I could just hear the air seeping out of my Career Plan A balloon.

There went the Oprah show, there went NBC—all in a matter of moments. Well, while I was putting my parents through my high school melodrama, I half-heartedly began to look through the other college brochures I had received in the mail. At that point, I really didn't care where I went; I blamed myself for missing what I *knew* was God's plan for my life. I mean, I just knew that God had called me to go to Northwestern and end up on *Dateline*.

Because I didn't have too much of a Plan B for my college career, I began to evaluate the other institutes of higher education based upon the pictures of the campus that I saw in the brochures. Now before you roll your eyes (though it might be too late already) and put down this book, let me show you how God orchestrated everything.

As the deadlines for non-Northwestern college applications drew nearer, my parents were pressuring me to decide which colleges and universities I would apply to. Well, I was still sort of pouting, and hadn't given much attention to sorting through the college materials. But, among the stacks of brochures I had was one from Southern Methodist University in Dallas. I had never, ever heard of SMU, and didn't have any desire to be in Texas. All I could remember was the humidity that I had endured during summers of travel there and to Louisiana and Oklahoma.

But I really liked the architecture of the buildings on the campus. I *really* liked them. And I thought that the brochure was put together well. I already knew I wasn't going to Northwestern, so why not apply there? I applied to SMU and a few other universities. I was accepted to all of them, and had no affinity toward one over another. I liked the location of some better than others, and I knew more about some than others, but I didn't really have a preference.

Well, I come from a praying family and my mother encouraged my brothers and me, as she frequently did (and still does), to pray and seek direction from God. Well, I did. I really didn't want to be somewhere God didn't want me to be, but since the Northwestern disappointment, I didn't have a passion to even broach the subject with God.

A few days later my mother asked me again where I had decided to go. I let her and my father know that I had finally made a decision: I would attend Southern Methodist University in Dallas, Texas. Okay, so maybe my response was more like, "Well, I guess I'll go to the one in Dallas..."

Regardless of my response, I set out for Dallas toward the end of that summer and found out that *the* T. D. Jakes was there. He had just relocated to Dallas from West Virginia the year before. Immediately on arrival in Dallas, I knew that I wanted to attend church at The Potter's House.

I began to attend church there and got involved in the Angel Tree ministry, a ministry that gives Christmas gifts to children whose parents are incarcerated. I also began to participate in the adult drama and dance ministry. It was there that I met a young lady who was from my father's hometown. As we began to discuss our family backgrounds, she asked me what brought me to Dallas from Albuquerque. I told her that I was attending SMU, pursuing a degree in broadcast journalism.

Wonder of wonders, she happened to work in the television department at the church and asked me if I wanted to be an intern there. Now, I was still trying to find my way to NBC, ABC, or something ending in *C*, and though I had watched Bishop Jakes in the years leading up to my high school graduation, I hadn't even considered the fact that there was a department of people working on his TV shows. But for some reason, I said yes to the internship. Not long after that, I met the director of the department and began interning there the summer after that school year.

It was the end of my sophomore year at SMU. Because I was a broke college kid, I also had two other jobs in Dallas while I participated in this non-paid internship. The internship went well, and by the end of the fall semester of my junior year, I was offered a part-time job with the ministry. During this time, The Potter's House was under construction, and a new worship center was being built on its campus. The church's building fund program, entitled "Hand Me Another Brick" was underway, and someone in the church's administration had requested that the television department produce promotional television spots for the giving campaign. For some odd reason, my manager assigned me, the new part-time employee, to produce these spots.

Truthfully, I was excited and terrified. I have always put a great amount of pressure to succeed on myself, and I didn't want to be a failure. So I did what my mom recommended all of those years: I began to pray. There were times when I would literally lie on my face before God and ask Him to give me *His* concept for these spots. I knew the gravity of building our building. God's people needed a comfortable place to worship, and we all needed to pitch in to make that happen.

Well, God gave me a few concepts, and I worked with one of the newly hired editors on them. We worked days and late nights in preparation for their airing. The first one aired on February 13, 2000. I remember that Sunday morning as if it were yesterday. I was preparing to go to the first of our three morning services when the Holy Spirit stopped me. I was at the sink in the restroom and I clearly felt the direction of the Lord to stay there in my campus apartment and pray. I looked at myself in the mirror, wondering how it could be God's will for me to *not* go to church.

But I stayed there and began to pray. As I did, the Lord began to tell me that He was about to change my world forever. From that day on, He would orchestrate the events of my life in such an amazingly clear way. In my normal oblivious way, I noted what He said, but didn't understand the gravity of it. Finally, I headed to church.

I arrived at church just before the second morning service, and went to the television control room, where my manager told me how much he and the congregation liked the spot. He said that Bishop Jakes seemed pleased with the spot as well. I was relieved with my manager's report and so I relaxed, satisfied that the spot served its purpose.

The next thing I know, Bishop Jakes appeared—or at least that's how it always seems. Bishop Jakes has a commanding presence that fills the entire room and, though I don't even think I was watching the door, it's as if I felt him enter the television control room. When he did, he began to rave about the commercial I had produced. How effective, how well produced, even how classy it was. He asked my manager who produced the spot, and my boss indicated that I had. Puzzled, Bishop Jakes looked at me and said, "You?" I nodded and smiled a half-smiley, half-scared smile.

Anyone who knows me knows that all of my teenage and adult life I have looked about seven years younger than I really am. I'm sure Bishop thought that there was no way that this fifteen-year-old-looking kid could have done what they're saying he did.

He was impressed and I was scared. I looked up at the tall Bishop Jakes and thought back to what the Lord had told me just a couple of hours before. Could this be the beginning of what He was talking about?

Apparently, it was. Since then, I have had the pleasure and the blessed opportunity to produce shows, commercials, conference services, and television series for Bishop T. D. Jakes. I've gotten to interview some of today's most profound and inspiring preachers, singers, and doctors, and I have met some great people. Even better than that, I've been touched, healed, and blessed by the people of The Potter's House and the ministry of Bishop Jakes. And it all started because I had given of my time to the Lord.

I was committed to the music and fine arts ministry. Then I was committed to working hard and doing a good job on my internship. Then I gave my all to producing the "Hand Me Another Brick" spots. I was blessed by my giving.

Now, I wasn't perfect; remember I didn't even want to go to Dallas at first. But God knew where He wanted me to be. I've made my share of mistakes, pre- and post-Dallas, but one thing that I believe has worked in my favor is my giving of my time, finances, and my gifts and talents whole-heartedly to the Lord. Not to Bishop Jakes, or to SMU, but I gave them up to the Lord.

I gave it UP, and began to give on a level that brought me before great men and women of God. And now, I wouldn't trade one minute of time and wisdom from Bishop Jakes with four years of working on the set of *Oprah* (no offense to her, of course!).

It's amazing, really. Because when I give unselfishly, I automatically begin to receive. That's right, good measure, pressed down and shaken together, God has caused His men and women to give right back to me time and time again (Luke 6:38), and I've never regretted my gifts to the Lord. They've brought me before great men, and I've begun to be fruitful and multiply.

Once you unselfishly, even cheerfully, begin to give of yourself in areas of your life where doing so is challenging and sacrificial, God sees to it that others will pour back into your life in exponential ways. After all, He's called you to be fruitful and multiply, so it's only His way to give you a pressed down, shaken together, multiplied blessing for your labor. Remember, God is not unrighteous to forget your labor of love (Hebrews 6:10). He will cause you to begin to multiply in ways you never dreamed possible—as long as you give it UP to Him!

And God Said, "Give Me Back My Life!"

◦ *Genesis 2:7* ◦

I ATTENDED A FUNERAL THE OTHER DAY. It was a joyful occasion; one of God's soldiers "went on to receive his reward," as old-school, seasoned saints used to say back in the day. He was an associate pastor at our church, The Potter's House. He was sixty-three years old when he died, yet Pastor Amos Sanders, the oldest associate pastor at the church, had left us suddenly.

We knew he had previous medical difficulties, but many of us thought he was all better. So as a significant portion of the church membership and volunteers traveled to Atlanta for what would be our first Mega Fest event, Pastor Sanders was the pastor who stayed home to hold down the fort. He had taken our other associate pastors to the airport for their flights to Mega Fest. And I understand that he even dropped his own son off at the airport as well. Later on that day, after taking pastors and family to catch their flight to what was being called the biggest Christian festival ever, before the sun would even set, Pastor Sanders himself would take flight—suddenly—to what is truly the largest Christian festival in all of eternity.

Pastor Amos Sanders went to heaven. While we were preparing for a great move of God on earth, God's great Spirit moved him right into eternity.

Our church family loved him. He was a spirit-filled man. We can never live with someone or look over their shoulders twenty-four hours a day, but what we saw in Pastor Sanders was clearly indicative that he had a strong relationship with God. And he was old school too! Pastor Sanders would end his prayers with a spirited, old-school whoop, and I loved it! He loved God and God's people. He would worship and praise God with little restraint in our services, which made an impression on me.

I didn't grow up in a church where we saw men, particularly men from his generation, worship with such abandon. I remember the last Wednesday night Bible class we had while he was living. Bishop Jakes played a bit of a song from one of his new CDs, and there Pastor Sanders was, sitting on the front row, with his hands extended and his face toward heaven. Even then, Pastor Sanders looked so peaceful, and it seemed that the glory of the Lord was just enrapturing him.

I truly admired him, and I'll never forget him. He taught me so much from afar. He taught me that you can take care of your wife and family, overcome physical hardships, support other men of God, and be kind to others. More importantly, he taught me that real men do worship God.

I've always been a worshiper. I remember as a youngster at about three or four years old sitting in church next to my father. That day, the choir was singing. Whatever they were singing struck a cord in my heart, and I suddenly began to cry. My father quickly asked me what was wrong, and I suppose I answered something, but I doubt at that young age that I really could communicate what was going on.

But looking back, it was my acknowledgment of the presence of God. Yes, I was a weird child. And though I played my share—quite unsuccessfully, I might add—of kiddie sports and classical piano, I never excelled in anything like I excelled in what Dr. Rita Twiggs, associate pastor of The Potter's House, calls "practicing the presence of God."

My connection with God at a young age was not coincidental, and I don't have any regrets about how ardent I was about my walk with God as a child.

The other day, I was remembering how my mom would ask my brothers and me how much time we had spent with God that week. I would come up with thirteen or fourteen hours for the week and my brothers would laugh at me and say I was lying. We have made total peace with each other about our childhoods, so there's no harm done there. I *was* wacky as a kid—and maybe as an adult too! But as I thought back and realized that the reason I was so insistent that I had had that much time with God is that I never did just count "prayer" as we call it as my prayer time. I counted my singing, my playing, my writing to God, and my directing that outstanding invisible choir in my bedroom. All of it I counted as time spent with God.

And though no one else understood me, and I didn't even have that clear of an understanding of myself then, God knew, and He also knew that I would come to understand it better myself one day.

> *The question is,*
> *"Whose life is it,*
> *anyway?"* ☺»

I'm so thankful that God allowed me to meet Pastor Sanders. And though I never had a conversation of much magnitude with him, I never had to. His life, his display of passion for the Lord, taught me to understand myself and even my childhood. I didn't have to know his whole biography to know that we were "men of like passions," as Paul puts it. Our love for God is so strong, and though people may not have wanted us to express it, we did, and still do.

Pastor Sanders put me at peace with being myself. In a world where we often see women worship so vehemently, he told me— with his life, not with words—that strong men do worship, and after that, they take care of business. And just like the large number of hours I would count as my time with God, all of that still counts as worship.

My time in church is not my limit on how much I worship God. My singing in the choir was not my only worship time with God. Genesis 2:7 makes it clear that when we were made, God breathed the breath of life into us, and that's made us a living creature. God's breath is in us. That's why we're alive. Then He commanded us to "be fruitful and multiply." The only way to do that is by using His breath to accomplish whatever He wants us to accomplish here on earth.

So the question is, "Whose life is it, anyway?" The Bible tells us that we're not our own, but we're bought with the price of Jesus' blood (I Corinthians 6:19–20). John 15 tells us that we didn't choose Him, but He chose us!

Right now, I'm traveling on a business trip. And this morning, as I awoke in my hotel room, I remembered a dream I had from the night before. In the dream, I was hustling and bustling around trying to do my job, and trying to sing in the choir, but I was never on time. My boss wanted to talk to me, but I wasn't around to talk to him. By the time I got to his office, he was on another phone call. I made it to the choir stand but missed rehearsal and had to learn the song on the spur of the moment. I had been distracted by people and things and had forgotten to do some important things on my job. And while God's grace and mercy kept me, I learned the songs, and nothing catastrophic happened in regard to my job, I was disappointed that I had not done all that I could have done in many areas of my life.

As I woke up, I asked God, "What do I do?"

His answer to me was, "Give Me My life back."

That statement sounded strange to me until I remembered Genesis 2:7. I'm alive because of God's breath. This life is not really mine to live. It's God's.

And when I take a lesson from Pastor Sanders, if I make everything that I do, in word and in deed, worship to God, I have a relationship with Him that's unlike any other.

It would have been impossible for Pastor Sanders to support a wife and seven children without working. Yet, his walk with God was so strong. I believe that it was strong because his communion with God was not limited to prayer, praise, worship, preaching, or teaching. But pursuing God's purpose and following His commands is worship. And when it all comes together— the prayer, praise and worship, and the pursuit of purpose—our lives become worship.

My friend, I encourage you to give the life that you have left back to God. It's His, anyway. You won't spend every day in the synagogue, and every waking minute won't be on your knees in prayer. Expand your definition of being a true son of God and realize that while Jesus had times set aside for prayer, He was also very much about His Father's business. Dedicate your purpose, your job, your family, and, yes, your whole life to Him and see just how fulfilled you'll be. Make your life one of worship. Whether you're male or female, God's life is in you. That means that we're using His breath for things that we shouldn't. But as long as you're breathing, there's still a chance to make a change for the better.

As Pastor Sanders put it, "'The steps of a good man are ordered by the Lord,' but you never know how many you're going to take." It's true. Each of our human lives, at one time or another, will expire, just like Pastor Sanders's did. But with our lives given to God in everything we do, we'll fulfill our assignment and leave behind an unmistakable legacy for others to follow.

That's the way to be fruitful and multiply. It's the Pastor Sanders definition of "Total Praise and Worship."

"'The steps of a good man are ordered by the Lord,' but you never know how many you're going to take."

-Pastor Amos Sanders, in an interview with The Potter's House in June 2004, shortly before his passing on June 21, 2004

God Knows My Heart! But…

≪ Psalm 1; Genesis 1:26–27 ≫

GUESS WHAT? I was never made to fail! Genesis 1:26–27 tells us that man was initially created to be like God. The first man and woman were created in His image. When I was growing up, some well-meaning Sunday school teachers would tell us that God made us in His image—therefore, no one is ugly! We all look like God! Well, quite frankly, you and I both know that that's not the case. We all have imperfections, physically and otherwise. No matter how cute you think you are, or how unattractive you think Jethro Jenkinstein across the street is not, there are some things in all of us that could stand a little work.

So what does being created in God's image mean? John 4:24 emphasizes that God is a spirit. He's an entity that can't be detected by the natural senses alone. He's a spirit. So when man was made in His image, we must know that it is our spirit that most reflects His likeness. It's our inner man that expresses the striking resemblance between the Maker and His masterpiece.

This is what lets me know that I was never created for failure! I was made in God's image, and it wasn't just to be cute! It was only when God breathed the breath of life into me that I became a living soul. And it was that part of me, the God-part of me, that was made to have dominion over everything around me.

I was made to rule over the fish, the birds, and the animals. I was made to rule over *everything* around me. I could eat the chickens when I wanted, and I could eat the fruit from *almost* every tree!

Well, you know what happened. Man ate what shouldn't have been eaten, and the sinful nature was introduced into the heart of mankind, putting our eternal souls in jeopardy.

I believe that because we submitted to something in the earth, the three-part man was set at odds against himself. His soul, where his intellect and will exist, was left to choose between what his godly spirit wanted and what his earthly flesh craved. I think this is why our flesh is challenged; when we chose to seek after the things of this earth, we unknowingly made a pledge of allegiance which stated that, in our lives, the things of the earth are to take precedence over the heavenly things of God.

When man chose to eat of the tree of the knowledge of good and evil, all of God's creation was put up for auction to the highest bidder and Satan won out in many ways. That's why he's called the prince of this world. Before sin entered into the picture, the things of the earth were the things of God.

The things of the earth can be used for good or bad. Money isn't bad, but it can be used for horrible purposes—and it can be used for beneficial causes as well. Sex isn't bad either. But it's only great in God's eyes when it takes place between a man and his wife. Legalism entered the church when we deemed certain things to be evil, rather than admitting that it was our motive and intent for using them that brought evil results. And because we struggle with the things of this earth, we tried to appear pleasing to God by refraining from eating certain foods, wearing certain clothes, driving certain cars, or earning certain amounts of money.

These rules really don't please God; they only please our flesh. Well, guess what our flesh is? It's just another thing on the earth. Our flesh was actually made from the dust of the earthly ground. We can't please God with it alone. Now that sin has entered the earth, our flesh doesn't contain any good thing (Romans 7:18)! No matter how I dress it up, oil it down with olive oil, or starve it, it is still susceptible to sin and earthly pleasures that have no eternal gain!

Have you ever wanted to please God so badly that you tried to do all of the so-called "spiritual" things? You may wear the long-sleeved shirts, ankle-length skirts, never cut your hair, never grow a goatee, use Vaseline as a substitute for make-up, and say all of the most spiritual phrases to the people around you. You may follow all of the rules at your church ("don't wear this color or hairstyle") while everyone is walking around (with close-toed shoes, of course) singing, "Praise the Lord!" to each other.

When we chose to seek after the things of this earth, we unknowingly made a pledge of allegiance which stated that, in our lives, the things of the earth are to take precedence over the heavenly things of God.

Though we may be grinning and enjoying Jesus, halle-lu, and aiming to please God, we're still forming fatal addictions, hiding secret pleasures, and masking ungodly flaws with religious mumbo-jumbo.

Why do we do this madness? Because we hate to fail! And just like the Colossians did (check out the "Trial & Error" section), we've tried all of our carnal remedies and employed our unsuccessful human effort to succeed at pleasing God. We've settled for just *appearing* to be pleasing to God, all the while saying to our co-dependent cohorts, and ourselves, "Well, God knows my heart..."

Yes! God does know your heart's intention to do the right thing! He's the One who actually put it there! It is the hidden man of your heart that desires to do right in the sight of the Lord. So, yes, that's correct. God knows our hearts. As a matter of fact, He disregards outward appearances and judges us by our hearts (1 Samuel 16:7). But we've got to take it a step beyond displaying that pitfall hall pass in the school of failure and excuses.

God knows our hearts, and He wants to use it as the motivating force to make some issues right in our lives. "God knows my heart!" This statement is only a pacifier for a failing soul that's crying to do better, aspire higher, and achieve greater.

We know the right thing to do (though sometimes we pretend to be confused about it), but often choose to do wrong.

Paul put is this way: "The good that I would I do not: but the evil which I would not, that I do" (Romans 7:19).

This man, who wrote most of the New Testament, is saying, "Hey, I struggle too."

Paul, who revealed God's plan for the church, said, "Sometimes I don't get it right." You remember Paul, right? He's the one who told us about spiritual gifts. He also said, "I can be a horrible person sometimes."

Evidently, Paul walked with God. God used him mightily. But, Paul sometimes messed up. And even though he, too, made mistakes, his response to his mess-ups was not, "Oh well, God knows my heart. He made me and He'll rescue me and deliver me when He gets good and ready." His solution wasn't, "Well, I'll just keep on praising God." He didn't blurt out a bunch of religious jargon and hide behind antiquated "church-isms."

He admitted that his imperfections and unrighteousness stopped him from being all that God had called him to be. He acknowledged his own weaknesses but capitalized on his strength: the crucified Christ who lived in him.

In Philippians 3:10–14, Paul sets his goal—to be more like Jesus and lay claim on all that Christ has won for the believer through His death, burial, and victorious resurrection. Paul tells us that at that point, he hadn't been completely successful, but his goal was to continue to strive for godly maturity.

While working the altar, I once prayed for a young man who wanted to rededicate his life to the Lord, but had a drug habit to overcome. As my pastor preached, he said something that struck the young man: "You can't make a deal with God. Either you're coming to the Lord or you're not!" At that moment, he knew he could no longer make excuses or bargain with God, saying, "Well, Lord, You know I want to do better. I want to renew my commitment to You.

When I get myself together, then I'll come to the altar." He simply had to get up and come down to the altar.

Psalm 1 is riddled with promises of God's blessings. But all of these blessings are dependent on one thing: ACTION. We prosper and we bear fruit when we live by the Word of God and avoid ungodly people and situations. We can't sit idly by, resting on excuses while God's blessings for our lives lay unclaimed. We've got to DO something about our situations, rather than just pretend that all is well while we drown in the misery of unfulfilled destiny.

As you attempt to move past your excuses and masks and into the blessings God has for you, here are a few tips that help me daily. Let's use these in our lives, and together we can be fruitful.

> *A struggle is only a struggle if you're actually struggling.*

1. A struggle is only a struggle if you're actually struggling. A fight is only a fight if all parties are fighting. The moment you make excuses for why you're not winning and begin to mask your losses with legalism and flesh-pleasing rules, your struggle becomes a habit and your fight becomes nothing more than a good, old-fashioned beat-down.

2. There's a winner in you! God breathed His breath in you, and if you're a believer, then Jesus Christ lives within you—and He has conquered all things for you. Now it's up to you to allow His Spirit to have dominion over you—and by the discipline of studying His Word and avoiding any person, place, or thing that hinders your goal of becoming whole, you will prosper, bear fruit, and be blessed.

3. When you get tired of fighting, and you don't think that you'll ever succeed personally, financially, or in any other area, refer to tips 1 & 2. Keep on fighting, and victory will be yours!

It's time to bear some fruit! Drop the excuses and stop the charades! Struggle with your struggles and fight the enemy, knowing that you were made in God's image and failure is not your final destination. Success is yours!

I'm Chosen?
Are you sure?

Genesis 1:26–27; John 15:16

SO I KNOW THAT I WAS NEVER MADE TO FAIL. But I know that I sometimes do. And I also know what it feels like to feel worthless after I've failed my heavenly Father. As a matter of fact, I have felt that feeling so strongly, and I've been overcome with so much shame and worthlessness that I have doubted my calling and even my existence.

After failing God and breaking your own rules, have you ever asked yourself, "How could God ever find a way to use me? How can I even ask God to help me now?"

Well, in the midst of this circus of doubt and shame is a masterful ringleader: he is Satan, the enemy of your purpose. He helped you trip and fall—and now, instead of "sweet nothings," he's in your ear whispering "bittersweet nothings"! He's so masterful that his voice can be disguised to sound like the voice of your own mind. He knows just where to hit you to keep you in a pit of shame and low self-esteem. And if you don't watch out, it will almost feel good to stay there. He might even have you fooled into thinking that you're a good Christian by wallowing in your failures.

Before long, you'll find yourself participating in what I call "spiritual self-mutilation." You feel so worthless that you beat yourself up, defacing the healthy image that God beautifully designed. You slowly forget that you're fearfully and wonderfully made, and you begin seeing yourself as the lowest form of humanity, not worthy to be visited or used by God.

You'll disregard the fact that you were created to have dominion in the earth, and you'll settle for being dominated by weaknesses, failures, and proclivities toward ungodliness. Soon, you'll be convinced that you've forfeited your opportunity to serve the Lord. If I asked you if you resemble this description of a pitiful and misguided soul, you may not answer immediately—you may not even be able to recognize the *you* that you've become. It may be a hard reality to face, but take a good look.

What is wrong with this picture?

If you're dissatisfied with the *you* that you've become and you're wondering if you'll ever get yourself together, or you're wondering why you're still around at all, there's good news.

The you that you see is not the you that you've been created to be!

You've been chosen by God! In John 15:16, Jesus tells His disciples that *they* didn't choose to follow *Him*; He chose *them* to follow *Him!* The same principle is true for us. Just as God told the prophet Jeremiah that he had been chosen by God before he was ever born, you and I have been chosen and given a specific calling and purpose in the kingdom of God.

Each time God created something in the book of Genesis, He always talked about what He would create first. He had assignments for fish, animals, and man before He made them! God doesn't make anything just because He can—He always has a purpose for it in mind! And God had a specific purpose in mind for you before He formed you as an embryo inside of your mother.

This is a magnificent truth in light of the fact that God promised never to leave or forsake us (Deuteronomy 31:6). And He sent His Son, who is the same yesterday, today, and forever (Hebrews 13:8)! He knows all things, including the intents of our hearts, and though He knew everything about us when He made us, He still gave us a purpose and calling.

This means that God knew about every one of your hang-ups when He chose you. But He chose you anyway. He knew about each failure that would occur in your life. But He chose you anyway. He knows about your future mess-ups. But He chose you anyway. He knows about your faltering heart and your wandering mind. But He chose you anyway.

> *The you that you see is not the you that you've been created to be!* ❧

When you accepted Jesus as Lord of your life, you may have chosen to walk down the aisle of your church, repeat the sinner's prayer with a friend, or lift your hands to God in submission while you were all alone in the stillness of your bedroom. But it was HE who chose YOU! And because He chose you, and you've entered into the covenant of sonship with Him, He's agreed to take you—and all that comes with you—while He gives you grace, mercy, peace, and purpose to live a victorious life!

So stop acting like God didn't know what He was getting when He chose you! He knows more about you than you know about yourself, and He is, as the old saints would repeat, "well able" to handle your dysfunctions and dis-abilities. He hasn't canceled His contracted plans for you. He has chosen you and called you to be fruitful and multiply! I know that it seems like a really bad deal for Him, but God is the One who wrote the contract for the redemption of our sinful lives, and He's the only One who can cleanse us from our faults and give us purpose-filled lives.

So if you've lived to see another day, then that's a sign that there is still a purpose for your life. You still have a chance to reach for your destiny. But first there are a few things that you must do.

1. If you're actually living a sinful life—REPENT, turn away from your sin! Realize that your lifestyle is hindering God's purpose for your life, and, inevitably, hurting yourself and others. Know that the almighty God is able to strengthen your weaknesses and help you overcome habits, faults, and temptations. But you have to sincerely ask Him to do so.
2. Understand that you've failed God and no doubt will do so again. But realize that Jesus' blood cleanses you of sin and if you're a believer, you've been redeemed and now have the honor of being

dressed in the righteousness of God (1 John 1:7–9). What does all this mean? I'll start by telling you what it doesn't mean. It doesn't mean that you have a license to do anything you please. It means you have a "get out of jail free" card.

You can be freed from the prison of failures, guilt, and low self-esteem. You're free to walk in victory, knowing that God has redeemed you. Now, He's expecting you to aim toward godliness in each area of your life. As you do so, you'll be enveloped in His grace, and you'll experience the blessings of being forgiven.

3. Finally, know that being a blood-bought child of God doesn't mean you're perfect; it just means you've been forgiven. As you discover this profoundly simple truth, you'll begin a love affair with the Lord that will lift you out of the abyss of guilt and seat you in the right-eous sonship of God.

You've got some living to do! So get to it! Walk in humility before God, knowing that He has chosen you, and despite many faults, He desires to use you. Run life's race, knowing that He'll pick you up each time you fall. And rest in the arms of unconditional love, a love so overwhelming that guilt, shame, and self-pity can't paralyze the pursuit of your purpose.

Christ in You: Protecting the Investment

◦ Colossians 1:27; 2 Corinthians 4:1–7 ◦

WE KNOW THAT WE'RE PART OF A chosen generation. And that can be a challenge. When we received salvation, our spirits were the main recipients. Our souls and our bodies are secondary recipients of this grace, but it's our spirit that's saved. That's why Paul had to advise believers to walk in the spirit and not in the flesh (Galatians 5:16). Our souls still have the option to let the fully saved part of us, the spirit man, or the unsaved carnal man take control. And our bodies, well, they don't have a choice; whoever (the spirit man or the carnal man) wins the battle for our decision-making souls tells the body what to do.

And so, as believers, we're in an ongoing process of doing what 2 Chronicles 7:14 tells us to: "turning from our wicked ways," so that the Spirit of God can be active and dominant in our lives. The more we allow the Spirit of God to win the battle of control over our wills, the easier it is to hear and obey the voice of the Lord. As a result, we begin to produce fruit by abiding in the center of God's will for our lives.

We never approach this process easily. Our flesh resists the will of God, and our spirits resist the urge to do wrong in the sight of God. But if we want to be fruitful, we've got to change our perspective and stop looking at life as a struggle between doing right and wrong.

Personally, I've found that when I see my life as the mission for God that it is, it's easier for me not to get sidetracked. I know that I'm not my own and that I've been bought by the blood of Jesus (1 Corinthians 6:19–20), but sometimes, because I have the decision controls, I sure feel like I'm running things! But man was made to be led, and one way or another, we will be led. Either God will lead us, or we'll be led astray. It's quite simple. We move toward God or we don't. We may be stagnant or move away from God, but any move that isn't in His direction isn't good. Lack of movement can be just as dangerous as moving away from God's will.

Really, we don't move toward God as if we're without Him and we're trying to find Him. We're really moving in the direction of His destiny for us. Because we're believers, He lives in us. Paul tells us that Christ in us is the hope of glory (Colossians 1:27). In 2 Corinthians chapters three and four, Paul details his ministry as one that shines the light of the Lord (that light being the knowledge of Jesus) on anyone who will hear him. Paul humbly admits that this light was shone on him first, and that's why he's so adamant about showing others that same light.

As believers, we always have to remember that our lives are designed to touch others. When the old saints used to talk about ruining your witness or "standing in the way of sinners," you'd always get some image of someone telling on you when you did wrong. They'd threaten that your bad business would get out. But there's more to it than that. There is gravity that's placed on our lives in realizing that someone's life is attached to ours. More than that, someone's salvation is dependent on whether or not we can shine God's light where they can see it and eventually believe in Him.

The truth is that we as humans are powerful, and we can do whatever we want to do. We can choose to live mediocre lives and give a lukewarm testimony of what God has done for us, or we can walk in power. If someone offered us one million dollars to abstain from eating beef for an entire year, even if we ate beef three times a day previously, many of us could do it. Those that say they couldn't really can, but they have chosen otherwise. We do have the power within us to do anything, because we have Christ within us.

And because we have Christ in us, we have to protect that investment of the hope of glory that resides in us. Paul is careful to tell us that Christ within us is not the immediate manifestation of glory. It is the *hope*, the possibility, and inkling of glory. While there is that possibility of glory in us, God won't manifest His glory through us without our permission.

The Bible tells us that God is a jealous God (Exodus 34:14), and anyone who has been jealous before knows that sometimes the motive for jealousy is a desire for love, admiration, or recognition. God wants all of these from us. Because He's all-powerful, He could demand and force us to recognize Him as almighty and give Him unending worship. But because He's not like man, He won't force you to choose Him. Just like He gave Adam the choice of eating the forbidden fruit, God has given us a free moral will.

> *We always have to remember that our lives are designed to touch others.*

Instead of forcing us to choose Him, God places His Spirit, known as Christ, the hope of glory, within us, in hopes that we'll choose to let that spirit make us success stories in Him. But in order to do that, we have to choose Him. If He's in us, didn't we already choose Him? Yes and no. As Christians, we've got to choose Him daily, and that means we have to protect the investment that's been placed within us. We have to show Him that we esteem His commitment to us by being committed to Him.

We do that by protecting the anointing that's on our lives. That's what God wanted from Samson. He wanted Samson to protect the anointing that was on His life. But Samson chose another lover (Judges 16). How many times have we chosen another lover over God? I can't count the times I've placed people, places, and things above God. It can be in small ways, like using poor time management and not spending time in prayer and the Word of God like we should. Our jobs and families can quickly become the other lover in our lives. We are to love those around us as we love ourselves, but we have to love ourselves enough to protect the precious anointing that's within and upon us.

I could give three simple steps on how to protect the anointing that's on your life, but there is only one glaring word that leaps into my mind: LOVE. Love God enough to recognize that no one else can do what He's done in your life. Love Him. Let your heart fall in love with Him again. And as we've discussed, love will always dictate action. Then we can easily follow the words that Paul writes.

"Therefore seeing we have this ministry, as we have received mercy…" (2 Corinthians 4:1).

Right here, we see that Paul was mindful that God has been and always will be merciful toward us. We can't forget just how much God has done for us. And we can't forget to handle the weight and responsibility that's on our lives the way we should. God has been kind to us, kind enough to shine His holy light on our souls and show us the face of Jesus. We were in darkness, and God's light showed us Jesus. He showed us Jesus! We can't do anything to earn or compensate Him for such a great gift. But we can certainly try not to spit in His face! He showed us Jesus! Where would we be without Him?

So with that mercy in mind, Paul says, "We faint not." We can't give up on this fight with the enemy and with our flesh. We have a ministry to share the gift that we've been given with a dying world. God showed us Jesus, and we need to have "Show Jesus" written at the top of our to-do lists. And doing that means that we have to let go of the things that will hinder us from showing Jesus.

There's no twelve-step program; we've just got to love Jesus enough to protect His investment in our lives. Love Him in our walk, in our talk, and in our hearts. We won't be perfect, but our hearts will be with His, and His light will shine!

Pray this prayer: *Father, I'm sorry for the times that I've chosen another lover over You only to be reminded that You're all I need. Only You are worth the first fruits of my time, attention, and effort. Though I've hurt You, You still choose to use me to help others. Thank You for Your patience. It hurts me to know that I've hurt You, and today I make a decision to love You and to show my love to You by protecting the investment You've placed within me. Most of all, I vow to love You with my heart, until my actions follow and Your light in me can be seen.*

> *"Integrity is the missing ingredient. It's the weakest link in our Christian character."*

Bishop Alfred A. Owens

FACING YOUR OWN SUCCESS

*"Well, we made it out of that part! But there's something I don't understand. I don't like it when I make mistakes. But I didn't know that I would sometimes feel uncomfortable when I get it right! I can't win! Shouldn't I be enjoying this moment of success, especially after all of the pain I've experienced in my past? People sure are something: they don't like it when you're wrong, and they can't **stand** you when you're right!"*

There is a cost to being successful. You've paid for being wrong. Here's how to enjoy being right—even when you're the only one at the victory party.

What's Your Point?

◁◈ *Mark 3:1–5* ◈▷

JESUS IS ALWAYS OUR BEST EXAMPLE. Throughout the Bible, God allows us to see how to respond (and how not to respond) to life's circumstances. There are so many characters with which we can identify, but ultimately, we're to take our cues from Jesus. After all, we're joined to Him, we're in covenant together, and we carry His name as our own.

Jesus is our prime example, and when it comes to learning how to operate in the calling and gifting God's given each of us, it's always important to take note of how Jesus operated in His. He's the Head, and we're the body, and our actions should reflect that of a fully functioning person. The head, or central control station, should send out directives to the body and its members, directing and monitoring the body's functions.

As our Head, Jesus teaches us that we have to know why we do what we do. What's our point in life? What's the motivation for our actions? If you have a ministry, why do you continue to function in your ministerial capacity? If you're employed in a certain career, why do you choose to stay in that career? If you're deciding to get married, why are you doing so? For every choice you make, there is a reason and a motivation behind it. And the area of our destiny and God-given purpose is no different.

88

Do you know that there are people doing what they're called to do in life, but their motive behind it is wrong? There are doctors who are absolutely brilliant, but they're in the field for the money or the prestige or because their families expect them to be doctors. There are teachers teaching simply for reasons of power and control over others and paid summer vacations. Many times, we don't have the proper motives behind what we do, and even though we're called to operate in the role we've been placed in, our motives dilute our opportunity to be truly effective.

I believe the Pharisees land right in this category. They were the law keepers, and they eventually ended up being the watchdogs of the Jewish church. It's a shame, really, because every organization needs order. Anytime people are involved in any purpose-filled institution, there needs to be a system in place that helps maintain order, safety, and a functional environment. I have no doubt that the Pharisees did some good things, but somewhere along the way they turned into what we would call "bad cops."

In Mark 3, we see them in action, just looking for a reason to charge Jesus with wrongdoing. It's a dangerous combination to have someone in a position of authority who is intimidated. All through the Gospels we see these law keepers react to their intimidation of Jesus. Here they are, law keepers, sent to be a benefit to society, but they are so threatened by Jesus, they try to restrict His healing activity by finding simple technicalities, like healing on the Sabbath. John Mark tells us this short anecdote, and it's a common occurrence—the Pharisees and Sadducees don't like what Jesus does for the people. How could this be? Here in Mark 3, He has just healed a man with a withered hand. What could possibly be wrong with making someone's life better? They didn't even consider the fact that someone's life was changed, but they concentrated on the fact that Jesus had seemingly violated the Sabbath by working and being active on a day of rest.

First, they clearly didn't understand who Jesus was, because they would know that Jesus was doing more work by having to tolerate them, than He was by allowing His virtue to heal a man. If Peter and John could heal a man simply by allowing their shadows to pass over him, surely Jesus, who bestowed that power to them, was all the more potent, and His acts of healing were all the more effortless! So is healing someone on the Sabbath really true work for Jesus? I think not!

Jesus was just being Himself, operating in one of His main roles as Prince of Peace, bringing wholeness to those who allowed Him to do so. But the Pharisees didn't understand that, because they had no real spiritual discernment to understand who Jesus really was. They were simply intimidated by Him.

"Anybody can be ordinary!" –Dr. Jill Waggoner ⏵⏵

As it is with the Head, so will it be with the body of Christ. If you ever get a chance to operate in your particular calling, be prepared; there will always be someone who is threatened by your gift. They will be intimidated, and will not even take into account the fact that you have been effective in your environment. They will be so intent on stifling your movement in your gift because they are fearful that perhaps they won't measure up. The Pharisees were supposed to be the highly esteemed people in the community, but when Jesus came, He stole the show!

Now, please take note! He didn't come to steal the show! He came to give us abundant life (John 10). But one thing I've learned is that excellence will always cast a shadow on mediocrity. Leaders will always rise to the top of the heap, no matter where they start (ask Joseph—Genesis). And the anointing will always steal the show! Get ready for it, but don't make stealing the show your goal. You'll turn into a pirate on the ship of your purpose, and only God should be the captain of that ship. You're really just a shipmate, doing what He says to do, when He says to do it. Don't try to steal the show.

On the other hand, you must learn what your point is. Jesus asked the watchdogs some very important questions in Mark 3:4 (NIV):

> Jesus asked them, "Which is lawful on the Sabbath: to do good or to do evil, to save life or to kill?" But they remained silent.

He wanted the Pharisees to realize what the point of His actions was. He wanted them to realize that their intimidation and fears could hinder people from receiving the help they desperately needed. Unfortunately, they didn't real-ize it. As a matter of fact, in verse 6, they became so incensed that they began plotting on how they could kill Jesus.

That might stop some of us. But Jesus knew His point, and as His body, we have to know ours. You are a gifted, anointed, and talented indi-vidual. And you've faced opposition, when you were just happy using your gifts to help others. But you've got to make a decision. You have to know the reason why you've been gifted the way you have. Jesus could have let the man with the withered hand continue to live the rest of his life handi-capped. If He were like any one of us, the opinions, comments, and plots of the Pharisees could have stopped Him from reaching out to help some-one whose life would never be the same after his experience with Jesus.

You can't give up, stifle your gift, and be intimidated because others don't like what you do. You have to examine your motive, and decide that it's better to do a godly thing, to save a life, to help your brother, to go the extra mile, not because you want to steal the show, but because someone's life will be better because of you.

Think of it this way. How dare you deprive someone of what's inside you, when you didn't place it there anyway? Is it better that you feel better about yourself and have the validation of others, despite the mandate that God has placed on your life? Are you so tired of ridicule that you've decided to "lay low" at the expense of someone else's healing? Don't allow the enemy to make you miss the point! God has called you for a reason, and someone is depending on your gift! Don't apologize, don't hide, don't back down! Someone needs you, and the enemy's camp needs shaking.

And don't be afraid that the haters are going to try and kill you. They won't get you. Remember, Jesus finally had to set the record straight. No one took His life; He laid it down! And just like our Head, the haters won't get you unless you let them! So get back in the saddle, and get to the point. Someone needs you! Walk in your gifting; someone will be blessed when they eat of your fruit, and God will take care of your haters.

So What?

WHEN PAUL WROTE HIS LETTER to the Romans, he communicated several truths about righteousness, justification, and the believer's position in the kingdom of God.

One important theme throughout the book of Romans is that Jesus died for Jews and Gentiles alike. Essentially, no one is exempt from receiving the promise of salvation. Though God chose the Jews to be the nation through whom Jesus would come to the earth, His death, burial, and resurrection were for all men.

At the end of the second chapter of Romans, Paul declares that physical circumcision was not an indication of being a righteous man or woman of God (Romans 2:28–29). Even if a Jew is physically circumcised, he may as well not be if he is not living a godly lifestyle.

Likewise, if a Gentile is uncircumcised but living a godly lifestyle, it's just as if he were physically circumcised, because his heart is circumcised.

These truths tell us that it's what's spiritual that really matters. Our works don't guarantee us a place in God's kingdom; our hearts do. However, our hearts should drive us to live a life that's pleasing in God's sight. Paul said that the Jews actually hindered the Gentiles from becoming sons of God because their actions didn't line up with their talk. They claimed to be moral, upstanding, law-abiding citizens, but they didn't practice what they preached (Romans 2:19–24).

It's always important to remember that when we say the name of Christ, people are watching the things we say and do. The enemy is always trying to discredit the gospel, and oftentimes, he seeks to use God's people to do it. We wear the right clothes, quote the right scriptures, but our lives (and our hearts) are far from the place that God has called us to live.

But, even if some discredit the gospel by their actions and their lack of faithfulness to God's commands, does it mean that God's Word isn't true? Does it mean that there really is no power or validity to the Christian faith? Paul tells us in Romans 3:4 that no matter what people do, God is absolutely faithful to His Word.

When everyone is lying and participating in ungodly activities, though they say they're not, God is still true to His Word. When people have left their post and shirked their responsibility, God has never and will never forsake His Word.

Remember, the enemy is always seeking to discredit God's Word and people. Sometimes He seeks to discourage God's people from receiving the promise God has spoken to them. To this, Paul's question and answer in Romans 3:3–4 still applies:

"For what if some did not believe? shall their unbelief make the faith of God without effect? God forbid: yea, let God be true, but every man a liar…"

There have been times when people have not believed in the gift of God that was within me, nor the promise that God had spoken to me. But this verse has encouraged me during those times.

People can say hurtful and discouraging things, and because we've been trained since infancy to respond to the affirmations and the dissent of others, we can stop ourselves from seeing the glory of God's will for our lives. We believe their words, and decide that maybe we can't overcome, or perhaps we don't have the ability to succeed. Maybe we shouldn't try to better ourselves economically, intellectually, or spiritually.

I've heard people say that there is no way to live holy, so we may as well do as we please. But let God be true and every man a liar! There is a way to overcome temptation, there is a way to achieve, and there is a way to reach our dreams!

Paul is saying to the Romans, so what? So what if you don't have the support of people? So what if you don't have the vote of confidence you'd like to have from family or friends? So what if people live ungodly lifestyles and try to find scriptural evidence to justify their actions?

It is God's Word that's true. Remember, it's not the earthly factors that make the difference in your life. Human approval can't cause you to fulfill your destiny any more than being circumcised can guarantee your admission into heaven.

> *Don't make your decisions, diminish your efforts, or base your goals on the temporary words of a temporal human being!* ☺

So what? When it's all said and done, we've got a Word from God, and His Word is what formed the earth. So surely, it's His Word that's more powerful than persons, places, or things in the earth. He is obligated to His Word; in the beginning all that there was *was* the Word. And the Word was with God, and the Word was God (John 1). So when you hear a Word from God, it's up to you to stand on the Word.

Communicate more with God than you do with man, and His Word will become more valuable to you than the words of mortal men. Sooner or later, you'll see that man's word is fleeting, but God's Word is the most absolute form of truth that we'll ever be exposed to. No matter if it seems that man's word is coming true, remember heaven and earth will pass away (Matthew 24:35). Man is made of earth, and just like this earth, man—and his word—will pass away too. But God's Word will last forever. That's what matters.

So what? Don't make your decisions, diminish your efforts, or base your goals on the temporary words of a temporal human being. Get in the face of God and decide that what He says is what really matters.

When You've Got It,
You've Got It!

Romans 10:2

A FEW YEARS AGO, I graduated from college with my undergraduate degree. The first year after I graduated I was excited to be able to begin saving money to buy a new car. The car I had no longer worked and I didn't have any transportation. I rode the bus, the rail system, and hitched rides when I could. I really wanted to have my own reliable transportation.

Once I got a full-time job, I began to save for a car. I wanted to pay a significant amount of money as a down payment, so my payments would be lower. Not only that, but my credit was questionable and I was a first-time buyer without a co-signer. So I needed to pay a lump sum that was larger than normal.

Well, I saved and I saved. And by God's grace, someone felt led of the Lord to contribute to the Kenneth Car Fund! At long last, with the money I had saved and the monetary gift, I finally had a significant amount of money to offer as a down payment and I was able to get my car.

Well, what if, after I'd already saved enough money, I just continued to feverishly build my savings and even accept the financial gift from the generous donor without ever going to purchase the car? I would be really excited about all that I'd saved up and all that was given to me, but I'd still have nothing to show for it.

That's just what Romans 10 describes to us. Paul tells us that the Israelites respected God and were even excited about religious things. But their enthusiasm wasn't based on what they knew about God. They didn't understand that they could receive salvation freely, so they continued to work hard for something that was given to all men as a free gift! That doesn't make much sense, does it?

Here they were, running a thousand miles an hour trying to win a race that had already been completed! Today, believers and non-believers alike work very hard to gain the approval of God. And really, people from either category may be classified as "good people." But, in order to enter into the kingdom of God, all that we really need is faith.

The people of Israel were religious people and they enjoyed practicing the customs and traditions of the Jewish faith. They were devout and conscientious about the rituals of their religion. But somewhere along the way, they started to think that it was their customs, rituals, and traditions that made them true children of God. They became excited because they thought that by following every precept of the Jewish faith, they would be able to earn God's righteousness and favor.

I believe that there is an intrinsic need and desire in all people for righteousness. Most people want to feel as though they are good and moral people, acceptable to those in authority. Most of us want to feel good about ourselves and to feel like we're nice, upstanding people. So we try and give to charity, save kittens from trees, and attend church every now and then. And because we shout "hallelujah" on Sunday, we feel good about ourselves. These seemingly selfless, quite self-serving acts just give us a feigned sense of righteousness.

The question is, what exactly is righteousness and how does one obtain it?

True righteousness is a gift from God. Righteousness is our admission ticket into God's kingdom. We get this ticket by giving our faith. Our faith is in Jesus and His blood, which has paid everyone's way into the kingdom. The problem is, not everyone knows that they can just give their faith in exchange for righteousness from God.

Saved or unsaved, no one can earn, work, toil for, or buy the righteousness of God. You either have it or you don't.

If you don't have it, it's because you haven't received salvation by believing in your heart and confessing with your mouth that God sent His Son, Jesus, to die on the cross for your sins. He died, was buried, and rose on the third day as a sign that we, too, though spiritually dead because of sin, can live resurrected lives. If you believe and confess that, then you are saved. You are a Christian, a believer.

After that, guess what? You have done all that you need to do in order to receive righteousness. Your faith has gotten you righteousness.

None of us can work for it, and really, we'll never be good enough to deserve it. As a matter of fact, the Word of God tells us that our own righteousness is just as good as filthy rags before God (Isaiah 64:6). And careful study tells us that these are not just cleaning rags, used to dust the house. I won't discuss the meaning of filthy rags, but the point is that God is so kind that He allows us to believe in His Son, and His Son's blood cleanses us, and we stand in His presence free of guilt and shame. Most importantly, we stand before Him dressed in His righteousness, not our own.

Yes, we can have that warm and fuzzy feeling inside, but it won't be because we've worked our way into God's righteousness. Even better, we rejoice in righteousness because it is a free gift.

And as we receive this concept into our lives and our minds, we'll have a zeal and enthusiasm for the things of God, but we'll be excited for the right reason. I've often been excited about what God is doing in my life. In the quest to be who God has called me to be, I've tried to work feverishly to achieve the goals that He's placed in front of me. And truth be told, it does take work to walk with God and do all that He's called us to do.

But what I didn't realize is that no matter how hard I work or don't work, the real promise and purpose that God has ordained for my life will only be accessed and received by faith.

Just like righteousness, we can't work hard enough for it. We work hard because we've received it, not because we want to get it. We've already got it! And when you've got it, you've got it!

The same is true with our gifts, talents, dreams, and callings. We have to realize that just like righteousness, we have to receive the plans that God has made for our lives by faith. We can't work for them.

After all, they're God's plans, and if we believe that they've come from Him, we have to receive them by faith. Faith is the only way to get to God. Without faith it is impossible to please God, for he that comes to God must believe that He is, and that He rewards those who seek Him (Hebrews 11:6).

> *If you've accepted Jesus Christ as your Savior, you have done all that you need to do in order to receive righteousness.* ⏃⏃

In other words, anything that came from God must be received by faith because our perception of His existence is based only on faith. We can't see Him, so our faith has to touch Him. Our physical hands cannot.

So we can't work to touch Him. We can't work to get the best things He has for us. We have to receive them by faith. We're not zealous because of all the work that we do. Our work will get us nowhere without God's blessing upon us. Our zeal and our joy come from knowing that He has called us, chosen us, and given us everything we need to succeed in life.

Does this mean we can now lie back and receive God's promises without doing anything in the natural? Not at all! James tells us that our faith without works following behind it is dead. But the more I learn about God and His purpose for my life, the more I learn that the real work is trusting Him, obeying Him, and focusing on Him. All of these things require a spiritual connection to God by faith.

While writing this book, my plan was to record music as a way to encourage the reader and help people to begin times of devotion with God. Well, I haven't sung in years! And at first, I was terrified. I didn't want to mess up, waste time or waste money—and I really didn't want to make a fool of myself! But I was convinced that God wanted me to have music as a part of this project. It was by faith that I began the entire thing, the book and the music. And when it came time for me to record, I had to really use my faith to be confident as I sang in front of the mic. But this scripture in Romans helped me so much. I had to remind myself that if it was God's plan for me to have music with this book, He must have, in some way, given me the tools to do a competent job.

We have to believe that God will never lead us astray; we have to believe that obeying Him will bring His desired results for our lives; and we have to believe that He will maintain our strength, courage, and tenacity to continue in our callings, despite life's obstacles and distractions. Using our gift is so easy compared to trusting, obeying, and focusing on God. The real work will always be in the spirit, because that's where the blessing is.

People who are famous singers, in the Christian world or outside, say that the work is never getting on stage to sing. The struggle and hard work were behind the scenes, backstage when they had to use wisdom in business and patience for their time to come.

Christians who have achieved dreams in any arena admit that their real struggle in realizing their dreams was maintaining their connection with God and believing His Word despite their circumstances. And when all is said and done, they have realized that it is the sheer blessings of God that have gotten them where they are. It wasn't their work; it was His faithful fulfillment of His promise that made the difference. God's liberal blessings far outweigh anything that we could ever work for: salvation, righteousness, gifts, material goods, or otherwise.

And that's what I'm happy about. He gave me salvation and righteousness. And He's blessed me with gifts and callings. I've got it going on! You do too. And when you've got it, you've got it! Now there's something to shout about.

"My purpose is much greater than how people view what I do. So I must please Him in what I do. I must do it to represent Him."

Donnie McClurkin

SPIRITUAL WARFARE:
Knowing When and How to Fight Attacks on Your Purpose

―――――――――――――――

"I'm ready to pull out my weapon! My guns are loaded and I'm about to open fire! You'd better not stand in my way. I'm on the edge and I'm not taking any prisoners! I'm leaving no stone unturned, and the hunt is on for...for...what was I looking for again? Well, it doesn't matter; you'd just better not get in my way!"

We are in a battle but, geez, haven't we taken this spiritual warfare thing a tad too far? Before you head out to the shooting range, let's talk a little bit about what we're really aiming for.

Killing Daddy's Giants

1 Kings 1 & 2

THE TIME HAD COME for King David to die, and the kingdom of Israel was up for grabs, or so it seemed. David's sons, Adonijah and Solomon, were in line for the throne, but which one would claim it? Would it be the popular, older brother, Adonijah, or would it be his younger brother Solomon?

King David's assistants and his wife Bathsheba knew that King David had sworn that the kingdom would be left in Solomon's hands, but Adonijah had the support of the people. He had manipulated other servants in the kingdom, and they were going to find a way to give Adonijah his seat on the throne of the kingdom of Israel.

Adonijah was so bold, in fact, that he had thrown himself an "I'm-gonna-be-the-next-king" party, at which he planned to take what would be his rightful position as king. He was the eldest of David's sons, and as was the custom, the oldest male had the right to the inheritance, the birthright, and anything else of significance that belonged to his father. The oldest son was the new head of the house, and because David was king, according to custom, his oldest son was supposed to be king.

But God always has different plans than man. Man's plans always fail, and careful study of the Bible shows us that, many times, the first and the last brothers generally end up finishing in reverse order.

Though Cain killed Abel so that he could be first in front of God, he still finished last in God's sight. God had accepted Abel's offering, because his heart was right. Manasseh received the blessing of Jacob, while the older son, Ephraim had to become subject to him. Joseph was the youngest of his brothers, and he ended up ruling over each of them. David was the runt of the family, but he was anointed king. The first Adam failed God, causing the downward spiral of the entire human race, and had to be replaced by the Second Adam—we know Him as Jesus. And of course you know, we don't pray to God in the name of Adam; we pray in the name of Jesus. It's His name that is above every name, and it was His blood that broke the curse that the first Adam brought on us. There is a biblical significance in the first and the last brother.

Now does this mean that in contemporary society, the youngest sibling will always be greater than the older siblings? Absolutely not, but by this, we do know that the smallest, the most underprivileged, the lowest on the ladder, and the underdog are many times most likely to do great things in life if they operate in line with God's plan. They may be down and out in man's eyes, but the Bible says that God uses the foolish, the weak, and the disenfranchised to upset the plans of seemingly wise men (I Corinthians 1:26–31).

Such was the case with Adonijah and Solomon. Adonijah had man's approval, but Solomon had God's mandate. He didn't just have David's promise; he had the call of God. He was called to be fruitful and multiply as king over Israel. God had promised David that his seed would prosper if they obeyed the Word of the Lord, and it was very important that the right seed would take David's place on the throne of Israel.

This story shows us that God has a plan for everything He does. He didn't cause Solomon to be anointed king simply because He was God and the earth is His and He could do what He wants to do. He knew that Solomon was the man for the job, and because He chose Solomon for the job, He placed everything Solomon needed inside of him to be successful.

The successor to David's throne had some work to do, and the right man had to be in the position.

Once King David caught wind of Adonijah's plot to take the throne from Solomon, he immediately had Solomon crowned king. And in chapter two of I Kings, Solomon is already given some heavy orders. At once, we see that Solomon has his work cut out for him.

It reminds me of a scene from *The Godfather*, or some other mobster movie. King David is on his deathbed, and Solomon is at his side, listening to his every word.

In a low, raspy voice, David disregards the pain and discomfort of his physical condition and hands Solomon his marching orders. There were some enemies that he hadn't yet settled the score with, and it was now going to be Solomon's job to take them on. Solomon listens intently as David lists the people on his "bad" list, and tells him that if any of them make a suspicious move, Solomon had better "off them."

Intense decisions marked the beginning of his reign, and it was going to take a person with Solomon's strength, courage, and humility to land on the throne and begin to immediately run the affairs of the kingdom. There wasn't much time to adjust to the position, and as a matter of fact, the Bible tells us that Solomon established his kingdom by taking care of David's enemies. His role as king was accepted and respected once he eliminated his father's enemies.

In other words, in order for Solomon to make his own mark as king, he first had to take care of his father's unfinished business. God chose Solomon for this task rather than Adonijah.

The Lord knew what He was doing; that was for sure. Adonijah was too pompous, too manipulative, and too dependent on people to handle this job. He wasn't too smart either. After his father died, he still made one more attempt to take the throne from his brother, even after Solomon had already been anointed king. Adonijah's plan was to marry one of David's concubines. If he were able to do that, as eldest son, he would be guaranteed kingship of Israel.

Now, his brother Solomon was gracious and allowed him the opportunity to remain alive in Israel if he didn't make any more attempts for the throne. But his hunger for power wouldn't allow him to remain still and save his life; he just *had* to make this last attempt. And it cost him his life. This kind of rebellious, self-serving, and stubborn person wouldn't be pliable enough to do the work that God had for this king to do. Remember, Solomon didn't just take care of his daddy's giants, but he built a tabernacle for the Lord that surpassed any previous one in beauty, stature, and magnitude.

It's quite conceivable that Adonijah would have only built an edifice to his own glory, and not the Lord's. Whatever the case, the fact is that God didn't choose him to be king, and he should have rejoiced. After all, he had a brother who would build a lasting landmark for God and take care of Daddy's giants for him.

You see, King David was a great man; he killed Goliath, the giant from Gath, when he was a young man. He was a splendid warrior, a gifted psalmist—and he was quite the lady's man. But when he died, he left some unfinished business.

> *Even if you're last in man's eyes—or your own—you're definitely first in God's eyes.*

No matter how great our fathers are or were, they couldn't do it all. They couldn't reach every goal, complete every assignment, or kill every giant. Consequently, many of us have been left with the job of killing Daddy's leftover giants. I believe that in every family, certain sons and daughters have been given the mission to fight certain giants that have plagued the family for years. And if you feel like you're the only one left to fight for the family, don't worry; God has already equipped you for the job.

God chose you for a reason, just like He chose Solomon. Adonijah was so wrapped up in human acceptance, power, and prestige, that he wouldn't have depended on God to be an astute man of war. But when Solomon had the opportunity to receive anything he wanted from the Lord, he didn't ask for money, status, or any of the other earthly things that man equates with success. He asked God for wisdom (1 Kings 3).

God chose Solomon because He knew Solomon wouldn't be consumed by his position. He knew Solomon would only be concerned with his mission. And if the fight has been left in your hands, and your family is disjointed or not equipped to help you complete the mission, there are some things you should know.

First, don't get the big head and act like you're the Anointed One. Remind yourself that you serve the Anointed One and that you have to depend on His power to help you beat Daddy's giants. Don't lord your relationship with God over your loved ones. You may feel that you have to force God in their face because they may have rejected you, and all you've had to rely on was your walk with God, but don't do it. Don't look down your nose; God has called you to bring peace into the family and to keep the enemy outside of the family. You won't ever kill Daddy's giants if you're bringing confusion to the family.

We never see David mistreat the brothers who mistreated him. And when Joseph finally met up with his brothers after he became ruler, he welcomed them with open arms. Be the man or woman God has called you to be and walk in love—it wasn't so easy growing up with you either!

Also, you have to know that even though you may feel so unequipped to fight this fight, there is something that God has placed inside of you. Your ruddy exterior, low self-esteem, and knobby knees are just decoys. Others think you're weak, but on the inside God has equipped, anointed, and appointed you to fight this fight—and win!

So even if you're last in man's eyes—or your own—you're definitely first in God's eyes. Ask Him for wisdom, and never become consumed with the power that you've been given. It's for fighting, not for flaunting, and if you seek God's face, He'll teach your hands to fight—and win! Whatever the giant—anger, divorce, poverty, or low self-esteem—the Lord has appointed you to slay it. And with His help, you will be fruitful and you'll multiply the blessings that God has already given your family. But first, you've got to whip Daddy's giants! Go for it!

A Job Opening

Nehemiah 1:4, 11

WHEN I AWOKE THIS MORNING, I knew I had a job to do. I'm not speaking of a nine-to-five job. I have a kingdom-building job that transcends the boundaries of time—its impact supercedes any length of employment at any company. This job pays better than any Fortune 500 CEO can give his right-hand man, and its benefits are in and out of this world—literally! My Boss keeps better records than any time clock or company watchdog—and when I finish my assignment, He will retire me in style, and He'll give me more than a gold watch.

Yup, I work for God. Now, don't get me wrong—I do have a forty-hour-a-week job, and it's a good job. Actually, I enjoy my job. But it's my kingdom-building job that makes my life complete. My kingdom-building job is why I live; it's what keeps me going. I can remember when I accepted this awesome employment. I, like so many others reading this book, was like a modern-day Nehemiah.

You see, Nehemiah had a great job. He was the king's cupbearer. This job entailed more than taste-testing. He was an astute advisor to the Persian king, Artaxerxes, and had the duty of making sure that the king didn't get poisoned. This job had many benefits, as you may imagine. He was exposed to the royal and extravagant furnishings of the palace. He got to eat the best food, drink the best drinks, and enjoy the luxuries of the palace.

His job did have certain pressures though. For instance, if anyone *were* to be poisoned, it would be Nehemiah; he ate the king's food before the king himself did. Not only that, but you don't gain the job of trusted advisor to the king just because you're a great guy. And you don't earn the trust of the king because of your sparkling personality. Be sure of it, Nehemiah had SKILLS! And his many talents landed him a great job, but they often put him in harm's way too. Just one bad decision or one negligent act could not only cost Nehemiah his life, but also the life of the king and the lives of hundreds of people. He had a serious occupational hazard!

Nevertheless, he seemed to be successful at what he did. He was enjoying the good luxuries of the palace, and his life seemed to be functioning on "business-as-usual" mode. But really, his heart was in Jerusalem. He was concerned about the Jews who hadn't escaped captivity (Nehemiah 1:2–4).

When God puts purpose in your life, He also puts passion in your heart.

When he heard the bad news that their enemies were accosting the people of Jerusalem and that the walls of Jerusalem were torn down, he was grieved.

Imagine that! Here he is, living that lavish life in the Persian palace, and his concern was for the people of Jerusalem. Some people in Nehemiah's position would have forgotten about the turmoil of the captive Jews, and if they remembered, they wouldn't have cared anymore. After all, Nehemiah had a cushy job with the king. The state of Jerusalem could have easily been disregarded.

But when God puts purpose in your life, He also puts passion in your heart. And many times, He does so in the same way in which He guided Nehemiah to his destiny.

Passion was birthed in Nehemiah because these people were his countrymen. He had experienced some of the hardships the other Jews were experiencing. Although he had a seemingly wonderful position in the palace, his past experiences in Jerusalem were still a part of him, fueling overwhelming compassion for those who were afflicted like he had been. He had passion and compassion, and guess what? His cushy job actually came in handy, in more ways than one.

He was already skilled—he would have to have been in order to maintain his position in the palace—but imagine how those skills were sharpened during his time at the palace! His raw instincts and astute senses were cultivated, and he was being groomed for his purpose and didn't even know it.

His real job was revealed when he found out just how bad the conditions were back home. His brethren from Judah were the bearers of the bad news.

"Hanani, one of my brethren, came, he and certain men of Judah; and I asked them concerning the Jews that had escaped, which were left of the captivity, and concerning Jerusalem. And they said unto me, The remnant that are left of the captivity there in the province are in great affliction and reproach: the wall of Jerusalem also is broken down, and the gates thereof are burned with fire." -Nehemiah 1:2–3

Well, Nehemiah's passion and compassion collided, and he began to weep before God. He fasted and prayed and mourned the conditions of his people for days.

Nehemiah was so distraught that he was unable to fulfill his job duties satisfactorily. It was in Nehemiah's job description that he should have a pleasant demeanor when serving the king—*or else!* But the next time he reported for work, Nehemiah's mind wasn't on his palace duties, but on Jerusalem. And the king noticed Nehemiah's countenance (Nehemiah 2:1–2).

Now, what happens next is absolutely God-ordained! Instead of punishment, Nehemiah received grace—and favor! When he found out about Nehemiah's passion to help the people of Jerusalem, the king permitted him to take the job God had opened for him: he was to help the people of Jerusalem rebuild their walls. He even obtained letters from the king that would help the cause.

Many of our lives are like Nehemiah's. But many of us don't realize what the Lord is doing in our lives. He's designed it perfectly, really. Someone reading this very page has been attending to the humdrum routines of life. And nothing is terribly wrong, except there's a burning passion in your heart for people having difficulties with situations that you've experienced. And now, you can't settle with everyday life. "Business as usual" just won't do.

Well, there are a few things you should and should *not* do. *DO NOT* just up and quit everything! But cry out to the Lord in prayer and consecration. Many of us have failed to be patient enough to allow the hand of God to move in our lives. The moment we felt the call of God on our lives, we dropped everything and ran toward "Jerusalem's walls." But take a lesson from Nehemiah.

DO continue serving where you've been placed; after all, it's training ground for your real job. And at the opportune moment, the Lord will fling open the door for you to take the job you've been waiting for. Then you, like Nehemiah, will move with favor under the hand of the Lord, without burning bridges (if you read the book of Nehemiah further, he did have to go back to the palace!).

So, if you've had a passion-compassion collision, have no fear, the Lord will use you in some way in that area. He will mightily use your gifts and talents to bring victory to the lives, regions, and nations that the kingdom of darkness has oppressed for ages. But for now, prepare for your destiny with prayer and consecration. Don't be so anxious to enter the fight that you miss your prep time! You will be fruitful if you allow your walk with God to grow as He strengthens your skills. In due time, you'll be as Nehemiah, remembered "for good" (Nehemiah 13:31).

Get Low!

Nehemiah 4–6; Psalm 91

WHEN I WAS A CHILD, I used to watch cartoons in the morning. The cartoons I liked the most were ones with a hero who could encounter any obstacle and win. Some of these heroes would fall off of cliffs, step on ACME bombs, and catch bullets with their bare hands. I used to want to be that kind of hero, the kind that could take a lickin' and keep on tickin'.

But the more I grow as a Christian and the more I live, I've found that I don't want to be that kind of hero—always fighting everything and everybody. I don't want to be the type of superhero that will fight at the drop of a dime. Many times, we've been trained to go to battle for any- and everything. We somehow get a volatile mentality that demands we become indignant and quarrelsome at every petty incident and accident.

"Suzie Mae said you stink!" Ready to fight.

"Dude said you're tryin' to steal his woman!" Ready to fight.

"Mattie don't like your dress!" Ready to fight.

"Tyrone said his truck is faster than yours!" Ready to fight.

When we declare war over petty issues, we are playing right into the hands of the enemy. If he can hit our trigger and get us to fire off for effect just to let people know who's boss, we'll also expend vital mental, physical, and spiritual energy. Then, when the real war comes, we're either too exhausted or too consumed by the petty issues in life to really wage war when we should.

Not only are we unable to fight when it's actually time to do so, but when we go to battle over every little petty grievance, we become distracted from doing the work of the Lord.

The book of Nehemiah gives us a notable example of when to fight, how to fight, and when to continue working.

Nehemiah had received and answered the divine call to lead the Jews in rebuilding Jerusalem's walls. He had filled God's job opening, and like any God-given mission, Nehemiah and the Jews were met with opposition. But the Jews had a praying leader in Nehemiah, and he knew the value of dwelling under the covering or the shadow of the Lord.

Here's what happened. From the beginning, Sanbalat the Horonite and Tobiah the Ammonite were sent by the enemy to upset the work of Nehemiah and the people. As a matter of fact, as soon as the people agreed to "rise up and build" (2:18), they faced the scorn of their enemies.

Isn't it interesting that as soon as it is discovered that the hand of the Lord is upon you and that you've found favor in high places like Nehemiah had, there's always someone around that doesn't believe in your vision, and doesn't affirm your calling! Just as Nehemiah was getting started on his new job, the haters took their place on the stage! It's no coincidence that when you're getting good and geared up to run full speed ahead for Jesus—here come the haters— and they're NEVER silent!

But be sure of this: when you're really called to a great work, there will always be some sort of opposition every step of the way. There will be haters, fighters, and trash-talkers. But if you've really been called, it shouldn't matter. Don't be discouraged by the haters, and don't doubt your calling. Don't immediately take opposition as a red flag to quit your mission.

However, don't celebrate the fact that you're facing extreme challenges either. And don't use those challenges as the sole confirmation that you've been called of God and are doing His perfect will. Many Christians apply the "glory in tribulation" principle to their lives and mistake the hardship in their lives for God's will for their walk with Him. Sometimes, conflict is an indicator that you should change some of your modes of operation.

Whatever the situation, you can take the guesswork out of your life's circumstances and be sure that you're operating in God's divine order for your life by looking at biblical examples to see if some of the same elements of your life compare to the Word of God.

For example, there are several factors that tell us that God called Nehemiah. Here are a few:

1. His calling and mission related to something he had great passion for. He had a heart and burden for the people of Jerusalem. (Nehemiah 1:2–4)
2. The Lord granted his request and gave him favor with great men. (Nehemiah 2:4–9)
3. At the right time, the Lord made provisions for the vision with people and tools that helped fulfill the mission. (Nehemiah 2:18)

When God calls you, He gives you a burden for the mission He's called you to, He grants you favor with those who believe in your mission and can be a resource to you, and He sends provisions through the people and establishments that will help you complete the work.

And lest we forget, He also allows you to face opposition and hear the mouths of the haters and the trash-talkers, just so you will be forced to rely on Him to accomplish your goals. That way, you'll have to give Him glory for your exploits.

That's just how it was for Nehemiah. He had a burden on his heart, he had the endorsement of the king, he had people undergirding the vision, and, oh yes, he had the haters!

When Sanbalat and Tobiah first began running their mouths (Nehemiah 2:19), Nehemiah continued his plans to rebuild the walls. He strategically placed families (symbolizing strong units called together by God) in specific places to begin building.

This is another sign that you know when you're operating in the will of God for your life. God *always* gives a plan as you follow His direction. He may not give the entire plan, but the portion of the plan He gives will be a plan of decency and orderliness. Never in this story do we witness a "free-for-all, who-done-it-and-how-come" spirit. Again, if your mission is riddled with chaos, confusion, and conflict from the bottom up, check and see if you're following the plan of God for your life in the right season of your life.

As Nehemiah executed his great, God-given plan, the haters yipped and yelped, but Nehemiah kept building. They mocked Nehemiah and the Jews, but guess what Nehemiah did? He didn't grab his pistol—yet. He got low. He prayed!

Here is where we find the principle of Psalm 91 active in Nehemiah's walk.

Nehemiah elevated himself above the insults of the enemy by retreating to the secret place. In this place, the presence of the Lord, the enemy can't touch you! Arrows, famine, recession, and terrorism won't be able to stop your mission! Get on your knees, give the situation over to the Lord, and let Him handle it (Nehemiah 4:4–5).

> *He who dwells in the shelter of the Most High will rest in the shadow of the Almighty.*
> *—Psalm 91:1*

But whatever you do, don't stop building your wall! Sanbalat and Tobiah were sent by the enemy to distract the people, and at first, it didn't work. They didn't jump down off of the wall and go to fighting over a few insults and some heckling. They had a "mind to work" (4:6).

These preliminary distractions are designed to defocus your vision, to make you lose sight of your dream. Think about it. Where in your life have you spent valuable time and energy fighting situations and people that were no more a threat to you than a paper cut? Yes, it hurt; yes, it was annoying; and yes, you'd like for your little pinkie *not* to sting when you wash the dishes, but was it worth dying over?

Right now, take the time to ask the Lord to breathe the breath of life back into your dream, back into your will to live, back into your vision. Don't die over silliness—and don't fight over paper cuts! You've got work to do! You've got a wall to build! If you've found that you've given up on your dream, and have stopped building the wall God asked you to build, repent now!

Wipe your salted, tear-stained eyes, get your wall-building clothes back on, and get to work! And the next time you're faced with mockery, insults, and embarrassment, make sure that you get low and stay in your secret place. When you take refuge in the Lord, He overshadows you. And as the Hand of God was on Nehemiah, it will remain on you to finish the work God has already begun in you.

You stopped your work and began to fight. And when you tried to resume working, you were so exhausted and your strength was so depleted, that you're now on the sidelines or in the recovery room, too wounded to complete the work.

But I commission you to come out of that volatile warfare mentality and stop fighting over every little thing. I am convinced that the Word of God does *not* tell us to fight and go to battle over every challenge. Now, I know what you're thinking—*The violent take it by force! Our weapons are mighty to the pulling down of strongholds!*

Yes, yes, oh ye warring child of God. But don't forget our weapons are mighty *through* God! And moreover, our weapons are *not carnal* (2 Corinthians 10:4)! In order to win any battle in life, we have to resort to the power of God to pull down any demonic stronghold. Sometimes, that means that we can't take our normal fighting stance in every situation.

Sometimes, what we really ought to do is get low! Go into that secret place that He, the Most High, has already provided for us. This may really challenge your theology, but I don't believe that it's for us to plead the blood of Jesus and rebuke the devil over every inconvenience in our lives. All of these things are not against you, Jacob (Genesis 42:36)!

Some of the things that we're warring over are merely life's occurrences. Some of them are actually distractions to get us to stop rebuilding the wall. And though we may not want to admit it, many of the so-called "hardships" that we face in life aren't of the devil at all—they can more accurately be described as products of our own poor decision making.

Whatever the case, please know that much of what we fight is not worth our fighting; these problems can be solved by taking quality time in the presence of the Lord, where His wings and shadow can cover us and keep us out of harm's way.

The Lord wants to do most of our fighting. We will be fruitful! But we've got to get low and take time for personal prayer, praise, and worship. As you acknowledge Him in all of your ways, as you thank Him for what He's already done in your life, and as you worship Him for who He is to you, you'll find strength and, most of all, you'll find protection. This protection is so bullet-proof that you'll be halfway finished rebuilding your wall (Nehemiah 4:6) before you know it.

Your mind will be fortified with the presence of the Lord, and because you're walking in His divine will and dwelling in the protective covering of His faithfulness, He will cover you, give you a mind to work, and let you and every-one know that God's people are protected when they get low.

"I've never met anyone who succeeded by accident."

Bishop T. D. Jakes

SHEDDING YOUR PAST, BIRTHING YOUR FUTURE

"I've had a tough life. You would think that I would run from the pain I've experienced the second I had the chance. But somehow, I still have trouble letting go of my past. After all, it's all I've had to hold on to. And problems are all I've ever known. I can sense that God wants to do great things through me, but I can't get past. . .the past!"

You're standing in your own way. So make a move. Start with that big weight on your shoulders and in your mind. It's called. . .the past.
LET IT PASS!

I See Dead People!

✺ *Isaiah 6* ✺

GOD WANTS TO DO EXTRAORDINARY things through you and me. He really does!

Sometimes it's hard to believe, and we can't even imagine it in our finite minds, but God has infinite power, and He wants to show it off through us!

When we discuss the things that hold us back from seeing God's power work in us, one of them is our vision. We have two sets of eyes really. We have physical eyes, and we have spiritual eyes. Sometimes—actually, most times, these sets of eyes conflict, and we have to make a choice. Which pair of eyes do we believe? Which pair of eyes do we agree with?

Now, the Bible tells us to walk by faith and not by our physical sight. But, let's face it: that can be a very intimidating task. After all, I'm trained to believe the things that I see with my physical eyes. Every day I'm inundated with a range of physical images, and they affect what I believe about others and about myself.

The news media tells me what the state of the world is, and I believe it. Why? Not because I trust these news reporters whom I don't even know. I believe what they tell me because they *show* me what they're telling me about. I don't even take the time to consider what they're *not* showing me and telling me; I just believe what they did show me and tell me.

Did you know that there are so many good things happening in the world, and we don't even know about them? It's because our society is based on the negative aspects of life. We thrive on the difficulties, roadblocks, and perils that life throws us.

What about the good things in life? There are some great things about life, you know. But because of all that we see, we don't always reflect on the better things of life. Think about it. Compare the amount of negative rein- forcement you see with your own eyes every day, through the eyes of the media, and through the eyes of those around you, with the positive affir- mations you receive about life and the world. The negative outweighs the positive, doesn't it?

Our minds are hampered with the bad things in life, but the Bible tells us to think on the good things of life (Philippians 4:8). We're to set our hearts on God and His goodness (Colossians 3:1–3). Beyond that, Hebrews, the book of better things, tells us how much better our lives are as believers saved by Jesus Christ.

But why doesn't our physical vision allow us to dwell on the better things in life? We've been trained by other people, other traditions, and the things we've witnessed. We've been trained to see the horrible things in life, the deathly things of life. It's been happening for years, for generations. Our atten- tion and our vision have been focused on death. Anytime our attention is directed and focused on the works of the enemy, we have to know that our focus is on death!

The Scripture tells us that the enemy comes only to "steal and kill and destroy" (John 10:10). If we're focused on all that he and his cohorts are doing, we are focused on death. We've been trained this way for years! And when we focus on death, our minds become deathly. And as a man thinks in his heart, so is he (Proverbs 23:7)! We've become the living dead—even as believers. We've been trained to see dead people!

Our intense focus on deathly issues, situations, and traditions has reproduced death for us and our children, only giving us more death to focus on. But we've got to get past death and begin to focus on life.

The prophet Isaiah makes a profound statement in his Old Testament book.

Historians tell us that King Uzziah was actually related to Isaiah, even as close as his first cousin. It seems here that it wasn't until his cousin's demise that he finally saw the glory and the presence of the Lord manifested in his life. The sight of the Lord made him repent, for himself and for his people. The previous five chapters of Isaiah were filled with visions and prophecies of death, but at that moment, Isaiah's thoughts were turned toward life.

> *In the year that king Uzziah died I saw also the LORD sitting upon a throne, high and lifted up, and his train filled the temple.*
> *—Isaiah 6:1*

Isaiah's cousin, Uzziah, was actually one of Judah's greatest rulers, but pride and fleshly works consumed him. As a matter of fact, God striking him with leprosy, the most unclean skin disease of that day, illustrated his fleshly ways. His flesh was consumed by uncleanliness, just like his spirit had been. Uzziah thought that he could approach God on his own terms, and he assumed the role of a priest, offering up incense at the altar in the temple. His fleshly presumption caused his career to end prematurely and abruptly. As was the custom of the day, Uzziah was quarantined to a life of isolation until the day of his death.

This was an unfortunate occurrence; after all, Uzziah was a ruler known for doing great things in the kingdom. Surely Isaiah must have been devastated. His cousin fell prey to a spirit of pride, and the people of Judah suffered because of it. Uzziah's son, Jotham, took over, and the kingdom's affairs went downhill from there.

Isaiah revered his cousin the king, and his respect for him turned into idolatry. Idolatry affects everything we do, because we have begun to worship something or in this case, someone, who isn't God. Therefore, our motives change, our actions change, and our hearts turn to whatever we worship.

When Uzziah died, the spirit of idolatry was struck down in Isaiah's life, and finally, his attention was back on the Lord! His vision was focused and his heart was changed. He repented, and the Lord forgave him.

How many times in our own lives have we seen this happen? We respect a family member or friend so much, that before we know it, they've become an idol in our lives. We can't see God in all of His splendor. We only see death, we only speak death, and, consequently, our actions are always based upon deathly motivations and circumstances.

We won't be able to see the vision of the things that God wants to do in our lives as long as we see death. And we certainly can't see the glory of His presence, as Isaiah did, with idols still in the way. We can't worship Him with the opinions of others in the way. If we reverence the thoughts, actions, and opinions of others more than we reverence the Lord, we will never function in the full capacity that He has ordained. Isaiah was a prophet, and he had been functioning in his calling, but when he saw the Lord, everything changed for the better, even his prophecies.

He had a heart for God and His people, and he had a sincere desire to see the people delivered from their evil ways. He no longer spoke gloom, doom, and death over the people, but his desire was to see the mercy of God in their lives and the glory of the Lord revealed in the nation.

Until chapter six, Isaiah could only see the judgment of the Lord falling upon the people. He was so affected by their fleshly ways and their pagan practices that the function of his gift was limited! This is important to note because none of what he said in the first five chapters of his book was untrue. The people of Judah were wrong, and their behavior certainly merited the Lord's judgment.

But the moment he saw the Lord, his whole perspective was changed. He didn't just see the people's actions; he saw the presence of the Lord waiting to heal the people. He saw the mercy of the Lord longing to forgive them. And most importantly, he saw the coming of our Savior, Jesus Christ! His gift rose to a new level, and his vision turned from death to life!

Now notice this: it was not when Uzziah sinned against God that he got leprosy; neither did he receive it when he tried to offer incense to God. It was when the priests tried to correct him and he became angry that he was stricken with the deadly disease. All along, God had given him mercy, and it was his responsibility to repent of his sin. But instead of repenting, he became angry, and before he could leave the temple, leprosy broke out on his forehead. At that point, he was as good as dead. When a horrifying condition erupts at the head of a thing (whether it be the head of a church, company, home, or otherwise), disaster is soon to follow!

Sometimes when certain conditions plague another extremity, like an arm or toe, that appendage can be amputated. But when the head is cut off, the whole body suffers and eventually dies. That's what happened here. Disobedience was displayed in Uzziah, and the rest of the people connected to him followed his lead. The central decision-making system, the head, sent the impulse of godlessness to its members, the people, and led them astray.

The Lord had to sequester him from the people, so He could heal them. The Lord always holds leadership accountable first. Judgment begins at the house of God (I Peter 4:17), and the heads of God's house must always account for those in the house. The blood (and the lives) of the people is required of those in leadership. So when Uzziah led the people away from the ways of God by his example, God judged him severely. In the interest of the people, God will always remove wayward leadership so that His people can continue to progress toward Him.

So the Lord rejected Uzziah, and it was time for the kingdom to move on. But Isaiah was unable to recover, and when his cousin finally died, his sorrow moved him to turn to his only help, the Lord.

Perhaps Isaiah had been waiting for Uzziah to be raised up, healed of leprosy, or perhaps he was just grieved because he knew that Uzziah's reign was cut short. Either way, when Uzziah finally died, Isaiah had to have had some sort of closure and some measure of sorrow. He must have had the correct combination of both, though, because he had a life-changing experience with the Lord. And he (like us) was never the same because of it! He had to change his focus from the works of the flesh to the calling of the Spirit. His prophetic career was enriched, and people were blessed. Surely, he began to bear much fruit, and I'm sure you'll agree it did remain!

He ended up being one of the major prophets that prophesied the coming of Jesus. His vision had become so clear that he was able to fore-tell Jesus' life, death, and resurrection. To this day, his prophecies are commonly used as references in essays, sermons, and books.

The works of the flesh can keep us consumed with death and unable to produce life and fruit. As we witnessed in the book of Isaiah, death can stifle your gifts and give you a case of tunnel vision that will only lead to dead people and deadly works. But Isaiah had to pick up the pieces of his broken heart and move on into God's calling to be fruitful and multiply. After his cousin's death, he recognized that the season had changed, there was a new ruler in town, and God wanted to do new and great things for His people.

I ~~See~~ Saw Dead People!

IT IS SO IMPORTANT TO RECOGNIZE when a season has ended and our roles in life have shifted or changed dramatically. Joshua learned this lesson, and was able to be a hero for the wandering children of Israel.

At the end of Deuteronomy, we see the end of Moses' life. He was the human deliverer of the slaves of Egypt, and let me tell you, Moses was a *bad* boy! Though the Lord would not allow Moses or the older generation of the Israelites to enter into the Promised Land, there's no doubt that God still blessed Moses abundantly. Deuteronomy 34: 7, 10–12 tells us just how great he was:

> Moses was a hundred and twenty years old when he died, yet his eyes were not weak nor his strength gone...Since then, no prophet has risen in Israel like Moses, whom the LORD knew face to face, who did all those miraculous signs and wonders the LORD sent him to do in Egypt—to Pharaoh and to all his officials and to his whole land. For

> *no one has ever shown the mighty power or performed the*
> *awesome deeds that Moses did in the sight of all Israel.*
> *—Deuteronomy 34:7, 10–12* ☺☺

When was the last time you saw a hundred-year-old who could run like a teenager, and see with 20/20 vision? Moses could, and what's more, there hasn't been anyone alive since, who had a face-to-face relationship with the Lord like he had. There's no denying it; Moses had it going on, and when it was time to die, he had the best burial service anyone could ask for. God buried Moses, and his burial grounds have not been discovered yet.

What would it be like to have a funeral service with God officiating? Would angels sing songs of joy and peace? Would God give the eulogy? Moses may very well have had an official, stately funeral, but the Israelites didn't get to attend it. This would cause an extra amount of grief for anyone who didn't get to mourn with the remains of a passed, highly respected loved one. At least Isaiah got to go to the funeral and the repast for King Uzziah, or so it seems.

But the children of Israel didn't even have the opportunity to really say goodbye to Moses, and their next leader, Joshua, didn't even realize that it was time for him to step up to the plate and take the people into the Promised Land. Joshua had received an impartation from Moses, but because he didn't even have definitive proof of Moses' death, Joshua was forced to take his role as leader in an interesting way.

God actually had to be the One to tell him to assume his position and begin taking the Israelites into Canaan. God is precise. He does nothing by accident or coincidence, and He wastes no words. In Joshua 1, we see that the Lord told Joshua that Moses was dead (verse 2). Apparently, there was an element of disbelief, and perhaps even shock, in Joshua and the people. Though they had mourned for a period of thirty days, they didn't have the closure they would have, had they buried Moses themselves and participated in the other traditional mourning rites of their culture.

But as I said, God does nothing accidentally, and I believe He didn't allow all the traditional "stuff" to take place because He wanted to illustrate all the more that He had given them something very non-traditional to do. For too long the children of Israel had focused on what *was* and what *should* normally happen.

They were so entrenched in the traditions of slavery that a forty-day tour through the wilderness turned into a biblical version of Gilligan's Island. They were trapped in the wilderness for forty years, when they could have possessed the blessing that God had waiting for them in less than two-month's time.

But now, it was time to move and finally receive what God had said would be theirs from the foundation of the world.

Joshua didn't get traditional closure, and there was no earthly sign painted in the wilderness saying, "HEY JOSHUA! YOU ARE ENTERING A NEW SEASON! GET READY! YOU ARE THE NEXT LEADER!" He didn't get any of the physical signs because the Lord wanted to begin to train him to hear His voice. He couldn't look to Moses for guidance anymore. He couldn't wait for Moses to come down from the mountain and report what God told him. Moses was *not* coming back! Joshua had to listen to God's voice on his own.

All Joshua had to go on was the word of God. He didn't even have the pattern that Moses had. We know that no one else had a face-to-face relationship with God as Moses had, so Joshua didn't even have a visual assurance that he was hearing the right voice, and obeying the right command.

All Joshua had was His word. And guess what? That was all he needed. It was the word of the Lord that gave closure to Moses' death and assured Joshua that he was, in fact, permanently gone. It was God's voice that told Joshua to move and seek out a land. It was the leading of the Lord that told Joshua when to fight, when to pray, and when to praise.

Joshua didn't have a pattern, and for many of us, as we walk on our path to fruitfulness, there's no precise recipe and no earthly roadmap to show us how to go where God has called us to go. Like Joshua, all we have is a Word from God. And guess what? That's all we need too!

He'll do for us just what He did for Joshua, assuring us along the way that He will be with us (Joshua 1:3–7). And He'll give us the tools, the people, and the resources to complete the task. And most of all, He'll give us the Word, and it's up to us what we do with it. Just like God told Joshua in verse 8, if we speak the Word, think the Word, and do the Word, success is 100 percent guaranteed!

We don't have an archetype; we just have a WORD. And once we get our focus off of dying actions, dying people, and dying traditions, we will be free to focus on life and the Living Word.

John 14:19–20 tell us that we can't operate based on what we see. In these verses, Jesus told the disciples that even though He was going away, He would be in heaven with God, and better yet, still with each of them! Had the disciples based the remainder of their lives on Jesus' death, they would be like many of us—seeing dead people and focusing on dead situations. But because they chose to believe in the resurrection of Jesus, the Living Word, they gave Him a home in their hearts.

We can't concentrate on the deadly issues of life. Doing so forces us to reject the life that God wants us to live. We'll never be able to move on the Word of God, we'll never be able to see the unseen, and we'll never allow the Living Word to operate within us the way He wants to if we concentrate on death.

Isaiah had to see a new revelation of God so that he could give a word from God that was filled with life. Joshua had to hear the voice of the Lord and operate on His Word, so that he could bring the people to a new level of living. The disciples had to believe in the Living Word, in order to fulfill the calling of God in their lives.

As these mighty men and women did, so must we. Aren't you tired of giving your attention to death and dying? Do you want to live? The only way you'll ever be fruitful is to take your vision off of dead things, and begin to focus on the Living Word. He's the only One who will take you along the path that He's designed for you. What He has for you to do is so unique and so extraordinary that your spiritual vision must be on life. Your vision must be on the Living Word.

What's in the past is in the past, and we can't dwell on it. It's time to move on! Get on with life, and let the Living Word take you into your promised land of destiny, and then you *will* be fruitful and multiply!

"My Prophecy Is Greater than My Past"

⸌⸍ *Acts 16* ⸌⸍

I WAS SITTING IN CHURCH watching a dramatic reenactment of Jesus' crucifixion. It was a moving production, and the congregation responded well to
it. As the players depicted the several events leading to our Lord's painful
death on Mt. Calvary, I couldn't help but be moved to emotion. Whenever
I see a play centered on Jesus' sacrifice, I always think about how much
worse His death really was. I believe that it is more graphic than many of
the horror movies we've seen. I believe that even the recent motion picture
depiction of Christ's death, *The Passion of the Christ*, does not capture the horror and agony that our Lord suffered. The details that we read in the Bible
lead me to think that it was more horrific than we could ever display during a church service. And then I am humbled: Jesus did that just for me.

It's actually difficult for me to fully comprehend the magnitude of the
love that Jesus showed by sacrificing His life for us. I don't believe there are
words in the English language that do His magnificent deed justice. I know
that there are no real words that I can say to Him to tell Him just how much

I love Him for giving His life as a ransom for mine. What I can't say, I strive to live in service, but even that's not enough. And as much as I try to tell Him how I appreciate Him, what really can you say to a God so perfect? Yet, He longs to hear us sing, pray, and praise and worship Him. There's just something about words.

Words have always been a powerful force. Words play such a significant role in our lives that anthropologists say that if an object exists in a society, but it doesn't have a name associated with it, it really doesn't exist to the people in that society. For instance, most Americans only know snow as *snow*. But to indigenous people in arctic areas, there are so many degrees of snow that numerous names exist for what we only know as *snow*. Just attributing a name—a word—to an object gives it validation and significance.

Words have been and always will be an influential force. The written word is potent, but the spoken word has a power all in its own. According to the Bible, it was the spoken word that got us here. The first chapter of Genesis is riddled with proof that light, darkness, the earth, and everything else God made originated from the spoken word.

If we're made in his image like Genesis 1:26 states, then we have the same type of creative power inside of us. After all, he breathed the breath of life into man (Genesis 2:7), and if life and our environment originated from words, then the same potential is within us to change our surroundings simply by speaking a word.

Now, one way or another, we've all been shaped by words. The problem is that most of those words were negative. Words, spoken in fleeting moments of frustration, anger, and pain have shaped our environments, just as God's spoken words shaped paradise for Adam and Eve. The mouth speaks out of the abundance of the heart (Matthew 12:34), and faith comes by hearing (Romans 10:17), and as a man thinks in his heart, so is he (Proverbs 23:7).

As the play demonstrating the crucifixion ended, the audience rose to their feet in a standing ovation for the wonderful job the cast did in reminding them just how sacred the death, burial, and resurrection of our Lord really is. Later in the service, my pastor also noted how impressive the production was. He chuckled as he commented that the actors who play Jesus are always body-builder types with rippling muscles. He laughed as he noted that we

never see a chubby actor playing Jesus. His point was well taken and as he prepared to begin his message that morning, he said, "Let the plus-sized men say
'amen!'"

And immediately, I said, "Amen!"

Anyone who knows me can attest to the fact that I am in no way a plus-
sized man. I'm slightly over 5'7" tall and, while I'm in my twenties, I'm enjoying having a lower 30-something-inch waist. So what caused me to emphatically
agree with the population of men who were more robust than I? Words!

You see, when I was a child, I was chubby until I was almost sixteen years
old. You wouldn't know it to look at me now, but I was. When I hit what was
to be my teenage growth spurt (in which I grew a whopping six inches, leaving
me at a rousing 5'6" tall), I remained about the same weight and people began
to comment how "skinny" I'd suddenly become. Well, if I'm skinny now, then
I *must* have been fat earlier, right?

Now many say that I lost the "baby fat" that I'd carried for the first sixteen years of my life. Whatever the extra girth was, it didn't matter. All I can
remember are coaches who told me I needed to do sit-ups at home, and family
members calling me pet names like "Chubbs" and the like. Was anything wrong
with exercise at home or harmless affectionate names? Not really—except that
these incidences shaped how I thought of myself, even more than a decade later.

Looking back, I was by no means the most overweight kid in the neighbor-
hood in which I lived, but I was always self-conscious about my weight. Reality
and self-perception can be very different. But when we believe our self-perception over what's real, it becomes our reality. Now this is a very light-hearted
example, but we all have worse childhood memories that shape how we view
ourselves—years into adulthood. And our self-images are all shaped by *words*.
So what happens to us is that, even as children, perpetual cycles of failure and
success have been created all around us.

Someone says what he or she thinks about you, you believe it, and then you
become it. You then speak it and hear it again, further reinforcing that positive
or negative opinion about you. Before long, you've incorporated these characteristics into your personality and character. But it doesn't stop there! The book
of James tells us that the faith we've developed is dead if there's no action
attached to it. So in order to continue a perpetual cycle of pain in our lives, we

somehow fall into the trap of *acting* out the negative feelings we have about our-selves. And the cycle goes on.

Think about it! How many times and for how many years have you played a role that someone else has cast you in? Aunt Lucy said that you'd never amount to anything, and you're determined to prove her right! Mama said that you're just like your no good daddy, and those words ring out in your mind as you continue down the same path of disappointment that your father traveled.

> *The idolatrous history of his father's ancestry flowed through his blood, but the heart of his inner man pumped the redemptive blood of the cross.*

Well, there is a way to stop this seem-ingly endless cycle of monkey hear, see, and do. We can learn a lot from the New Testament character, Timothy. When we first encounter Timothy in Acts 16, we dis-cover that Timothy was the son of a heathen Greek father and a Jewess who was a believer.

Now, even today, in some circles, eyebrows raise at the sight of families comprised of various ethnicities. Well, back in Timothy's day, "mixed families" were a big no-no. It was said that any Jew who married outside of his or her race was bound to acquire infection and disease seasoned with a good dose of God's judgment! This was Timothy's situation. His father was a heathen and his mother was a Jew who had converted to Christianity. And the Bible is careful to mention that people in the community knew all about it! There's nothing like some nosy neighbors to magnify your problems.

Imagine that! Timothy was born into a catch-22. He had become a believer because of his mom's teachings, but there was a dark side of him that wasn't acceptable to the public. They spoke well of him, and many probably spoke well *to* him, but they also spoke of his heathen heritage. He was known as a kind person, but somehow his background disqualified him from serving the Lord. How could someone with such a tattered family history possibly be of use to God?

I'm sure that to some Jews, he was too Greek to be a Jew, and to the Greeks, he was too Jewish to be Greek. He was saved, but his sinful heritage hung over his head like a black cloud. The idolatrous history of his father's ancestry flowed through his blood, but the heart of his inner man pumped the redemptive blood of the cross.

Have you ever been in a catch-22? I think that every Christian has, whether they will admit it or not. I have. There's a part that loves the Lord with all of your heart, your soul, and your strength. But there's also that part of you that is caught in that perpetual cycle we talked about earlier. And the people around you like you, but because of shortcomings and failures, they seem to think that you don't meet the standards for successful living.

Some of us have participated in the several deadly sins listed on the church docket for dismissal from being an acceptable Christian (as if there's such a thing), fit for the Master's use. We've felt repulsive and undesirable because of a habit, the birth of a child out of wedlock, our appearance, or our family's background. We've felt as if an abortion, a broken law, or a broken vow has made us some substandard Christian who should have barely made it into God's kingdom, much less make the cut for service to God.

And though we know deep in our hearts that we are absolutely saved from the pits of hell, though we sometimes even question that, there's a suspicion that we'll never live down the details of our past. And what's worse, we've had to fight our self-doubt in the midst of a bunch of nosy neighbors, who claimed that they know all about our situations!

What may be the worst part of being caught in a catch-22 is that while you're anxious to prove to everyone that you're not what they think you are, you're deeply afraid that you just may be exactly what they say you are. This is a catch-22. I've been there. You've been there. And Timothy had definitely been there. But despite this catch-22, Paul chose Timothy to travel with his missionary company.

You *are* chosen! And despite your many catch-22s, God has placed people in your life who can see your worth to the kingdom. Paul was not concerned about Timothy's past; he was concerned about his future. Everyone has contradictions to their calling. Which will you focus on? You can be fruitful and multiply, but you've got to start by looking at what God has placed within you, rather than at what people are saying about you.

I Have a Prophecy!

❦ *1 Timothy 1:18* ❦

HOW TIMOTHY'S FAITH MUST HAVE WAVERED at the thought of actually seizing the opportunity to serve with a great man like the apostle Paul! Could he really rise to the challenge of being a missionary? Did the apostle Paul really know what he was doing when he chose him? What would happen if the others found out that Paul's most recent protégé had an ungodly mixed heritage?

What will happen when they discover that my father isn't a Christian? What if they knew that sometimes, I feel just like my father, so far from the Lord? What if they knew how much I doubt myself and my God right now? What if they decide they don't want me to travel with them anymore? Does Paul's acceptance of me really mean that God loves me? Does God really want to use me? I thought that I was unusable! If I say yes, will the pain of the past finally subside?

These are the thoughts that flow through the mind of someone caught in the grasp of a catch-22. But Timothy teaches us a powerful lesson, by choosing to take the risk of receiving more ridicule and rejection.

Sometimes, after enduring a lot of personal pain and public scrutiny, even the very thought of being the beneficiary of any more contempt will be the determining factor in making any progression in life. I know that I have felt paralyzed at even the mental suggestion of advancing in my career or pursuing personal relationships. The pain of the past was too prevalent, and it seemed safer to cower in the corner until the room of my life was empty of any bystander who may have wanted to mock me.

But I've learned that the only way to be fully healed from past pain is to defy the past and take the risk of seizing future opportunities for growth and success. Failure will never be behind you if you stay in the room with it. But that's just what we do sometimes. We may be successful in many areas, but we all have had areas in our lives that seemed too painful to address, even with God. When we fail to address the pain, we end up becoming roomies with our issues in the horrible house of pain.

We must take a lesson from young Timothy. He pursued God and the things of God. Please note that just service in the house of the Lord is not enough to secure healing from the past. It often helps escort us further away from our pain, but our ticket out of the house of pain lies *only in God's hands*. Paul's letters to Timothy note just how much Paul admired Timothy's faith and love relationship with God. Paul's remembrance of Timothy's service was secondary to the thought of his love for God. We must pursue a close relationship with God before dedicating ourselves to Christian service.

Our relationship with God will bring us to a place where we can be healed enough to serve, and have the courage that Timothy had to accept the challenge of becoming a missionary. But even after stepping out on that courage, the journeys weren't easy for the young missionary.

Throughout Paul's letters to Timothy, Paul had to encourage the sensitive, young missionary during his solo mission to Ephesus. Paul had gone to Macedonia and had sent Timothy to minister to the Ephesians. They had been to Ephesus before, but since that missionary journey, the Ephesians had been entangled in (of all things!) false teaching. Isn't it interesting that Timothy would be sent back to a place to tell people how to overcome false statements and perceptions about their faith while he was dealing with the same personal obstacle? He had to overcome false perceptions about his heritage and prove that God could still use him even though he didn't meet man's standards for service in ministry.

One of the first things Paul told Timothy is that he needed to operate in ministry according to the prophecies that were spoken about him. Now, let's take all of the spiritual spookiness out of the term *prophecy*. *Prophecy* in its simplest term is the declared, spoken word and will of God. It's not fortune telling or weather prediction. It is just God using a person to speak His words.

Paul was telling Timothy, "Listen, your past, your appearance, and your ethnic background don't matter anymore. You've been called to a higher position in Christ, and your mission must be carried out according to what God says about you" (1 Timothy 1:18, paraphrase).

And that's what we have to learn. People will always talk, but what really matters is the word that God has spoken about your life. He's the One who created you, and He's the One who knows your ultimate purpose. Let those words be the words that shape your world.

Further study of the people in Timothy's community and neighboring areas shows that they reacted solely to what they heard and saw. In Acts 13, they heard Paul's preaching and believed the gospel. But in Acts 14, some unbelievers (haters) came along and turned them against Paul and his group of ministers. Because of the haters, the people who had just been blessed began to get violent. Paul had to escape into Timothy's hometown, where a man was healed in his presence. The people there were so shocked at the healing that they called Paul and Barnabas gods, and fell on their knees to worship them. Meanwhile, more haters influenced those worshipers, and together they stoned Paul and Barnabas. Then, they dragged them to the outskirts of the city because they appeared to be dead.

Here's the point: people are prone to react to what they see and hear! More importantly, the same people who think they know so much are dealing with their own internal confusion and dysfunction! The same elated people who heard the gospel and rejoiced became a violent, uncontrollable mob in minutes. And the same people who fell to their knees in worship of Paul and Barnabas turned and attempted to brutally murder them. These were the people in Timothy's community. These were the people who, with their mouths, shaped how Timothy perceived himself.

Why do we heed the opinions of crazy people who try to tell us what sanity really is?

None of these people could properly perceive who Paul and Barnabas were. The truth is, they weren't gods, and they weren't the enemy. They were just ordinary people.

Sooner or later, we all have to realize that we are *all* just ordinary people, and that the only reason we can do the extraordinary things that we do is because God says we can. So allow His words about you to be the words that determine your destiny. The opinions of people can fluctuate quicker and more frequently than the stock market. But the Word of God stands forever.

> *Why do we heed the opinions of crazy people who try to tell us what sanity really is?*

No matter our shortcomings, failures, or weaknesses, when we begin to operate according to the words that God has spoken about us, we'll begin to fulfill the first commandment He gave to man in Genesis 1:28—*"be fruitful and multiply."* We'll begin to see His purpose for our lives fulfilled, and we'll learn that His words about us are the only ones that matter.

God values His word so highly that John 1 tells us that He *is* the Word! And Jesus is the Word made flesh (John 1:14). So when Paul charged Timothy to minister according to the prophecies or the Word of God that went on before him, I believe that he was referring to more than just the prophetic utterances of the presbyters. I believe that Paul charged Timothy to preach the Word of God and to do so with the Living Word of God before him. And the Living Word is Jesus Christ!

What makes the past fade into the past is the reality that Jesus lives within us and He is *the Final Word!* Any other words that have been spoken about us are null and void when measured against the potent words of Jesus. And He said that if we abide in Him, we can be fruitful in His kingdom; we can be of worth and value (John 15). He said that He has all power. And if He lives in you and me, then we must be powerful people too. But we have to realize that we have the power within us to break the cycle that words have created in our past.

It all starts with a Word. *The Living Word!*

Like I said, words *are* powerful. And God's word is the most powerful. God spoke His word about us, and then sent His Living Word to live in us, so that His word could come out of us and accomplish what He spoke about us! Now that's a cycle!

Make this declaration: *Today, I make a decision to watch the words I speak about others and myself. I choose to believe that what God says about me is true. Only His words will determine my destiny. I will allow those words, and the Living Word that lives within me, to shape my world. I can and I will accomplish all that He says I can. I will be fruitful and multiply!*

"Yesterday's in the tomb—today's in the womb. There is nothing I can do to change yesterday. Yesterday is over. But I do have a future ahead of me."

Paula White

GETTING TO KNOW YOU:
Protecting Yourself from Soul Invasions

———————————————

"I've never felt a greater calling on my life than I do right now. And I've never felt further from it. How do I move into what God has called me to do when I keep falling into traps of failure and self-sabotage?"

Yes, you have been called, but there's one thing you forgot to do: get to know yourself. Find out what's inside of you, what needs to stay, and what needs to go!

Fight or Flight?

Ephesians 4:27

WHEN THE ENEMY ATTACKS YOU, he comes against the place of least resistance to him. He may enter through little keyholes that may have originated in past generations and ages far back beyond your earthly years. Whether you've left an entryway for him, or one of your ancestors has, he takes whatever roots and pathways that have been left wide open because he's a deceiver and a cowardly lion. He roves, stealthily—seeking whom he may devour (1 Peter 5:8). He takes precautions to persuade and coax his way in. He enters into "unmanned territory!"

He plays on vulnerable affections in your life. These are untapped, unfulfilled places that long to be touched and attended to by God. He takes advantage of these weaknesses because he knows that these are places where you are least likely to resist him—and if you do try to resist him, you won't be able to for long. He knows that if you resist him, IT IS WRITTEN, he must flee. If he can infiltrate those places where you can't resist him, he's got it made!

That's why the Bible tells us never to give *place* to the devil (Ephesians 4:27). That means we shouldn't have places in our lives that are unmanned and unprotected. In order to protect the most vulnerable areas in our emotions or will, we must first recognize them. Many of us know some of our major struggles, though we may ignore them.

Even those of us who do know where we struggle may not know why we struggle in that area. Consequently, we end up trying unsuccessfully to police our actions, rather than allowing God to heal our wounded souls. Meanwhile, the enemy is on God's property, making a mockery of God's people and distracting them from the mission that He's given them.

Regardless of whether you know where you struggle or why, there are some key principles that will help you. The first and main key is the Word of God.

The Word of God is sharper than any two-edged sword. It's so distinct; it's tailored to every mechanism the enemy can try. It's formed and fashioned so that every situation that life places in front of you can be solved in one swoop. The enemy knows this. He knows firsthand that not one word that has proceeded from the Lord's mouth will be proven false. Not one word will return unfulfilled. It *must* perform those things it was *sent* to perform (Isaiah 55:11).

That's why the enemy seeks to discredit those who are *sent* to carry the Word of God. For many people, their faith is stifled and they can't receive the power of the Word when they have to receive it from incredible sources. The enemy knows that the Word must perform those things it was sent to perform, so he tries to demolish the images of those who are sent to deliver the Word, which has a 100 percent guarantee, and a 100 percent performance and success rate.

Faith comes by hearing the Word of God. How can people hear without a preacher, and how can they preach unless they're sent (Romans 10:14)? So, the ploy of the enemy is to make a liar out of the Word carrier. Who wants the product inside the box, when the box is already full of holes? Once the Word is delivered, received, and deposited, it must spring up full force—IT WILL DO what it was sent to do.

Many people are destroyed because of the lack of knowledge (Hosea 4:6). They won't receive the pure, unadulterated Word of God from an incredible vessel. Without the power of the Word with you, you don't have enough strength to fight the enemy; and if you don't fight—or resist—he doesn't have to flee. But once you submit yourself to God and His Word and resist your enemy, he must go. Then he knows he's in trouble.

You have to know the truth before you can really be free (John 8:32). The Lord is not deceitful like the enemy. He doesn't look for a way in. He waits for you to open the door and permit Him in—knowingly. He wants you to make a calculated decision to allow Him access to your life and let Him be Lord of it. At that point, He can do your fighting for you.

Your fight is to maintain a high enough level of faith that will allow God to go to work on your behalf. And how is faith received? It is received by hearing the Word of God. And the battle begins again as you learn what the Word says for every arena of your soul. And the fight intensifies as you begin to live what the Word says about your life. Believers must continually receive and use the Word of God. It is our weapon.

Once the decision to follow God is made, He can fight for you. You don't have to fight; the real battle's already won. Your fight is the good fight of faith. This fight of faith is the battle that ensues as you wait for the unseen promises of God to manifest and overshadow what the enemy is showing you in the world of seen circumstances and problems.

It's quite a challenge; we've been taught for so long that what we see is our reality. But truthfully, these are temporary realities. And while they exist for a moment, if we allow them to, these circumstances will have lasting effects on us, even after they've vanished.

How many of us have allowed loved ones who have come and gone to affect us? Their harsh words linger on and we never forget what they did to us. The enemy operates in our circumstances and tries to gain access to our souls. Our soul is where our will, intellect, and emotions dwell.

We are three-part beings. We are spirits, we have souls, and in this earth, we live in bodies. We discussed earlier that God is a spirit (John 4). If He created us in His image, then we are spirits too (Genesis 1). Our souls are the very human parts of us. We incur most of our damage in our souls. Our memory is in the conscious and intellectual parts of our souls and the horrible things that have happened in our lives are never forgotten. They are kept right there in our souls. This is a tragic circumstance, because our soul also holds our will. Our will is our decision-making force. We make our choices in our soul, where our will resides. Then our bodies just follow what our will tells it to do. Our will can follow the spirit or it can succumb to the circumstances that try to affect it in the flesh.

A prime example of how the combination of spirit, soul, and body works is the story of the fall of man. In the beginning, God chose to make man in His image, or His likeness. When He made man and woman they were in perfect communion with Him. As a matter of fact, the Bible tells us that the Lord walked with Adam in the Garden of Eden. Then Satan came, in the form of a serpent, and immediately began to try to infiltrate by affecting the circumstances— and he did so in the place of least resistance.

> *Neither give place to the devil!*
> *–Ephesians 4:27*

This is not a bash against women; this is a biblical principle. God placed Adam as the head and leader of Eve. So why didn't the enemy approach the leader? Because everything he does is out of order; he is not interested in operating in order. It shows his cowardice and his lack of power. Sometimes we give him too much credit. We are the ones who Jesus gave all power, and we often run around, afraid to yell too loudly or make too much of a ruckus because we don't want to attract any more attacks from the enemy.

We've got to realize that the enemy is not as strong as he appears to be. He's more sneaky than he is strong. We've given away much of our power to him, just by being paralyzed by fear. The Bible is clear when it tells us that God didn't give us fear (2 Timothy 1:7). The first thing that is listed in talking about fear is power. Fear paralyzes our power. We are more powerful than the enemy. When we're defeated, it is often because of our lack of knowledge of who the Word says we really are.

Jesus told Peter to be sober and vigilant because the enemy was seeking to defeat him and sift him as wheat (Luke 22:31). He's seeking to do the same to all of us. And he does so through the place of least resistance.

In the Garden of Eden, he came to Eve while Adam was not present, and began to tempt her through her circumstances. He offered her the fruit that God told them not to eat. His reasoning for tempting her to eat the fruit was that her circumstances would change! She would be better if she disobeyed God. As a matter of fact, she'd be more like the God she loved if she ate the fruit (Genesis 3:4–5). Is it obvious to you how the enemy can affect our circumstances and our pervert affections to defeat us? He didn't go to the leader or the head of the team, because it was easier to get the response he desired by starting at the bottom of the chain and working his way up.

That's just what he does with each of us. Jesus and I are a team, just like Adam and Eve. But he never attacks Jesus; he always comes to me, and he tries to infiltrate my weakest area. In other words, he attacks the weakest area in the weakest place of his conquest. The saying is true: a chain is only as strong as its weakest link.

Again, it's not that women are weaker than men. However, God's plan places man as a covering and a leader for his family. It's really more of a responsibility than a power position. It's not a position of power to be wielded or hoarded; it's a role to be assumed and taken seriously.

Men should never act as though we are above women, because when it comes to the team of Jesus and me, even as a man, I'm definitely the weakest link! And when the enemy comes to attack my winning team, he always gets in through me, and not Jesus! That's why I have to rely on the Word. I get fuel to fight the good fight of faith from the Word of God, while God fights the battles I can't win alone.

I fight to stand. I fight to walk in the unseen, without letting the seen distract me while the enemies in the unseen whoop me. I have to fight to keep my mind in a state of what reality really is. I've even got to fight my flesh and myself. I have to fight long and hard enough to be around when the manifestation of the victory that God has already gotten for me comes.

When it comes to fighting, I have to fight proactively and reactively. I have to strengthen myself with the Word of God and feed my soul the Word, especially in the places where I struggle most. Those are the places where I'll be attacked first. Then I've got to react and use the Word for the places that have already been attacked or are being attacked right now.

Yes, I've got work to do. But it's all for a good reason. I've got to bear fruit, and I can't let the enemy's soul invasions stop me. I've got to protect the weak points in my emotions, in my character, and in my personality. And if I haven't identified those weaknesses yet—I've got to hurry and find them out!

Discovering Hidden Weaknesses: Finding Strength in Discovering Inner Weakness

≪ Psalm 19:12–14; Psalm 90:8 ≫

SO I'VE COME TO REALIZE that there are areas in my life that get me into trouble. Not trouble with the law or the government, but in trouble with God and man. The enemy attacks these areas constantly, and it always gets me into trouble. Sometimes, these places are so worn and weak, it's not much of an attack, because there really is no resistance. It's similar to thumping already-cracked glass. It won't be long until the glass shatters.

There was a time when these situations would cause me trouble. This type of trouble would interrupt what would be a normal flow of events in my day; it would buffet relationships and alienate me from people who love me, and cause further friction with those in my life who don't. As a matter of fact, the trouble that I would repeatedly find myself in occurred so frequently, it almost became the normal flow of events or occurrences in my day. I'd become so accustomed to dysfunction and distraction that I failed to even attempt to discover what caused me so much trouble in relationships with people and my walk with the Lord.

Now, you don't need to know which areas in my life caused me trouble! After all, I'm still discovering many of them myself. The truth is, it doesn't matter what the area is—it could be my mouth, my need to please others, my lack of self-confidence, my fear of intimacy, or my tendency to be manipulated by others. It could be a need for attention, a proclivity toward depression, or self-serving greed.

Whatever the area that plagues me and causes me to fall into the same situations time and again, I have them—and so do you! What's most important is that I discover what these areas are and find out what makes me do the things I shouldn't, while I leave the things I should do undone. Though I refer to these issues as ones that disrupt healthy relationships with God, friends, and enemies (yes, the presence of "the haters" can be healthy for me—ask Jesus; His haters helped Him receive a name that is above all others!), these issues, if left unaddressed, could certainly lead to trouble with the law or government. They can even be physically and spiritually fatal!

But before you find yourself physically or mentally imprisoned, or stricken with a terminal spiritual or physical illness, I'd like to share with you how I found answers to some of those areas in which I struggle.

In Psalm 19:12, David asks, "Who can discern his errors? Forgive [some versions say "cleanse"] my hidden faults." There are faults and mistakes that we make but are unaware of. These hidden faults David refers to here aren't ones we hide from others. These are faults that are hidden from our own vision! David asks for help for those known presumptuous and premeditated sins in the next verse. But first, he asks God to help with faults that he doesn't know about.

When I think of the word *fault*, I think of cracks and crevices in the ground, which geologists call faults. That's just how many of us there are! We are made of the earth, and we have cracks and crevices in our character and our souls that the enemy sneaks into. We've got to learn where they are, so we can guard them from the enemy, who already knows where our cracks are. The enemy knows, and many times, people around us know our issues too!

Actually, it's very possible that these faults are evident to those who are around us while they go almost completely undetected by our own radar! But there are ways to make personal progress and find out about these things that make us trip.

One way to find out what to do in a given situation is to find out what *not* to do. First, let's find out what you shouldn't do when searching to find out more about yourself. Don't ever fully believe your own press.

David knew about both good and bad publicity, and really, so do we. David stood in between lovers and haters as he made his rise to kingship. Jonathan loved David as he loved his own soul (I Samuel 18:1). But Saul, Jonathan's father, hated him and wanted to kill him. Now if two people from the same house can vary so drastically on their view of one person, there's no way that all of the people in your life will agree on their opinion of you. So don't believe your own press.

However, don't completely disregard your own press either. It can be beneficial to seek personal advice from individuals who not only love and care for you but will tell you the truth. But because they are humans who only see and know a limited amount of information about you, their advice will never be fully complete. Plus, their affection for you may cloud the entire truth about you. But their advice may steer you along the right path toward self-discovery.

Likewise, people who care nothing for you may offer a sound perspective about you as well. But it may be buried too deeply in harsh and hurtful statements for you to get any helpful information about yourself.

What you should do is ask the Lord to show you some of these hidden faults. Ask Him what makes you get into the same types of situations over and over and perpetuate the same cycles of pain. Take some time for self-assessment.

So many times in the church, we're confronted with people who seem to have a revelation on everyone but themselves. But God is calling us to look in the mirror! There's no way we can see what's wrong with everyone else, and not discern our own weaknesses.

In our everyday lives we look in the mirror regularly. So there shouldn't be reason for me to have to rely on everyone around me to tell me that my neatly trimmed fade has quickly become a nasty afro. I've already seen it in the mirror! But spiritually, we don't look in the mirror often enough.

It's never easy or painless to look in the mirror and see blemishes, spots, or wrinkles in our persona; but God calls us to do so. Before we, like David in Psalm 19, deal with the willful sins, we must first ask the Lord to show us the hidden things that cause us to stumble in our walk with Him. We'll find that these hidden faults and errors in our soul's foundation, if eradicated, will stop many of the cycles of willful, "presumptuous" sins in our lives.

> Let us therefore, as many as be perfect, be thus minded: and if in any thing ye be otherwise minded, God shall reveal even this unto you.
> —Philippians 3:15

Careful study of the word *presumptuous* can actually be troubling. Numbers 15:30 talks about punishment for "presumptuous sins." In the times when this book was recorded, these types of sins are those that are committed with what's called a "high hand." It's not necessarily the nature of the acts that set these sins in their own category; it's the condition of the heart when they're committed.

A short study of these "high-handed" sins reveals that they are done right in the face of God, as if shaking one's fist at Him. Have you ever said, "Nanny-nanny-boo-boo" and stuck your tongue out at God? I've never done it physically, but sadly, I have done it figuratively. It's the lack of the fear of the Lord, and it gets us in very deep trouble with Him. After all, He knows He's God, and in these types of cases, we fully know it too, and don't care!

It's almost as if we're saying to Him, "So what? Whatcha gonna do about it?" This area is one that should be marked in our lives, because anytime we take this attitude, a prideful spirit is sure to take root in our lives. We'll begin to think that we can challenge God to a duel, and we are so, *so* wrong! Pride comes before destruction (Proverbs 16:18) and it really is true: our arms are too short to box with God!

No matter the action, the text regarding these sins suggests that we don't even really care about the consequence that comes from them. We don't care about the hurt they bring God or others. We'll just do anything we're big and bad enough to, and "if God has any questions, you tell *Him* to come and see ME!"

This is so dangerous, but many of us have done this to God more than we'd care to admit. It goes further than trying God's patience; this is about defying His deity. If we really experienced the wrath of God in our lives, like the people of the Old Testament, we'd probably rather be struck with lightning three times.

But today, we've gotten so used to the "Grace & Mercy" message that we're willing to try anything and then have nerve enough to sing and shout praises in church on Sunday morning. (At first, I had written "sing and shout praises to God," but quickly erased the words "to God" because He said, "They're not singing and shouting to Me! They're singing and shouting praises to themselves! They have become their own God.")

My pastor, Bishop T. D. Jakes has a saying: "When self rules, the soul stinks!" And it's so true. The last verse in the book of Judges notes that without a king in Israel, every man became his or her own king and did what was right in their own eyes.

We've got some Kingless Christians today. It's not that God has lost any of His power, but we have to choose to make Him Lord and King of our lives. Then, He can cleanse us and put us back in our places in Him. This is where holiness allows us to "see" God, or enter into His Kingdom. It's not about getting into heaven; it's about being under His authority in the earth, and consequently assuming our own God-given authority.

But before we get back to that place, we've got to ask God to reveal the cause of these presumptuous sins. Sometimes we're angry and hurt with the Lord, and we don't even know why. It could be unanswered prayer, loss of a loved one, or failed hopes, dreams, and desires.

Many people fall into traps of sexual impropriety because they lacked a father growing up or they were molested as a child. People sometimes commit certain crimes because they were poor as youngsters and had to find their own way to survive in life. Still others hurt and manipulate people because they lacked discipline and love from their families. Then their attitude becomes, "Where was God when I was hurting? Why didn't He rescue me then?"

We thought God should have performed for us like a circus ringmaster, or worse, like the circus kangaroo that jumps through the hoop at the crowd's command. But God is not at our beck and call. He's absolutely God, and His sovereignty cannot be questioned. This may not be so comforting to those who are looking for solace about their past. But careful study of the Word of God lets us know that every person who is noted for greatness had a tragic past filled with hurt to overcome. Abraham, Jacob, David, Ruth, Joseph, and Job—oh, yeah, and Jesus too—had so much hurt to overcome in their own lives. But they all made sure to align themselves with God's will and His heart. And though each made mistakes (except Jesus), they took the steps to be certain that they stayed in the will of God.

If you're reading this book now, and you're angry with God, stop reading and ask Him to forgive you for your anger and the acts that followed that anger. If you've been angry for so long you're not even sure why you're angry anymore, ask Him to show you why you're so angry, and why you hurt so badly. He will, and then He'll heal you from it.

When we take time to question ourselves and ask God to give us clarity and deliverance on these areas in our lives and hearts, He will! He'll begin to cleanse us and heal us, and it will make it hard for the enemy to force entry into our lives and our souls. We'll be able to fulfill the mission God's given us—to be fruitful and to multiply.

Paul put it like this:

As we press toward the mark, the Lord will show you—YOU (Philippians 3:14–15)! But we have to ask Him to. He'll reveal where the enemy gets into your soul. And if you let Him, He'll help you with your weaknesses. The healing starts right there.

Once we know about our hidden faults, we can ask God to fill them with His presence. Psalm 90:8 says that God has set all of our secrets before Him, and our inner weaknesses in the light of His countenance. The presence of the Lord will shine a light on the dark areas that need His healing. The light of His presence will fill the voids of insecurity, doubt, and shame.

Whatever we're longing for, or marred from, His Spirit can heal us. Healing is a lifelong process. We will always have issues to work on, and the enemy knows it, but that doesn't mean that we should be left unguarded while we receive healing from the Lord.

Remember Job? The enemy told God, "I can't get to Job, because you have a hedge of protection around him" (Job 1:10, paraphrased). We're just like Job.

God has put a hedge of protection around us, even though we're not perfect. Especially because we're not perfect! He protects us as we seek healing and grow stronger in Him. His love for us won't allow us to be devoured while we're on His Potter's wheel.

But we've got to be accountable to God as well, and commit ourselves into His hands for healing. True healing begins with accepting responsibility for our own progress. This doesn't mean that we have to take the blame for our condition, because many of us suffer from generational curses or childhood scars. But accepting responsibility for our own progress means not letting disadvantaged situations dictate how we'll live the rest of our lives. We started off on the wrong path through no fault of our own, but if we end up on the wrong path, that *is* our own fault!

We've been given access to the Supreme Healer, and it's our job to stay on God's operating table while He does major surgery. And that starts with exploratory surgery on our hearts. Ask the Lord to show you the cracks and crevices of your hidden areas of weakness. Then give Him permission to fill them, and as He does, you'll find strength to overcome the open sins that have tried to dominate you.

We cannot afford another season of unfruitfulness because we won't allow the Lord to give us the diagnoses of all of our diseases. We've got to let Him weed through our issues, and we'll come out with a plentiful harvest and a testimony to share with others.

Let It Burn!

✑ *1 Peter 4:12; Numbers 22 & 23* ✑

JOY BRINGS AWARENESS. I've often said that real joy comes from being in God's will and that joy is sensitivity to the Lord and what He's doing in our lives. There's often a joy that comes from knowing that God has chosen me. I have joy knowing that I can rely on Him, even when I'm quite unreliable. The old folks used to say, "I get joy when I think about what He's done for me."

In the Bible, joy is always associated with knowledge. James 1:2–3 (NIV) says it like this: "Consider it pure joy, my brothers, whenever you face trials of many kinds, because you know that the testing of your faith develops perseverance." The writers of the Bible often introduce joy into their conversation when the earthly circumstances they were discussing were anything but joyous. That's why joy is a fruit of the Spirit. It is something that's acquired through our relationship with God, despite our situation. Real joy comes when there isn't any earthly reason why we should have joy. When everything looks grim, joy comes in and reminds us what the Lord has told us about our situation.

As a matter of fact, joy only comes from being in the presence of the Lord. Joy doesn't come from getting a new car. Happiness does, however. But happiness is a fleeting pleasure. Only living in the presence of the Lord gives lasting joy.

Joy is a valuable quality because it gives us strength. I believe the Lord causes strength to flow through joy because the joy that He gives us often comes in the midst of hard times. Life's obstacles often force us to seek the Lord when we'd normally be relaxed in our relationship with Him. But when hard times come, we're driven to aggressively seek the Lord! It's our nature.

Those of us who really love the Lord and love to spend time in His presence in praise and worship do so because we've learned the value and safety of dwelling there in times of trouble. We can pretend that we just began to seek Him by choice, but really, some of the greatest things we learn from the Lord were learned during hardship, not times of great blessing.

I can personally say that some of the times when I felt I was "tight" with God were times when there was no other option. I didn't always choose Him like I choose a friend to hang out at the mall with. I'm sad to say it, but it's the truth. Quite honestly, I realized that I needed Him because I would mess my life up completely, even more than I already had. I began to seek Him because of my own personal failures. I became intimate with Him when it seemed as though the only other option was death. That's just the truth.

Though I've always enjoyed spending time with the Lord, I didn't decide to *aggressively* pray, study, and spend personal times of worship with Him because it was the right thing to do. I did those things because life was getting too tough, and I obviously wasn't a good manager in the job of my life. I learned so much about Him when I had to rely on Him to provide for my needs. I gathered valuable information when I had to depend on Him to keep me from losing my mind. It's not a sparkling testimony, but it's mine.

But in those times of prayer, praise, and worship, I would get the greatest sense of joy and peace, despite my own shortcomings. Many of the hurts I've encountered in my life were my own fault, and many were not.

I've also faced obstacles for being good at what I did, or for wanting to do the right thing. And honestly, sometimes those were the hardest struggles to face. I used to get upset because I couldn't understand why others would ridicule me for being myself. I hated when others rejected me because they were threatened by my talents—especially when I couldn't see all that God had gifted me with.

My desire was to be accepted by others, but I didn't want to do so at the expense of failing to be who God created me to be. But oftentimes, I couldn't have both. I used to wonder why I was always challenged in one area or another, even when I didn't do anything wrong.

I couldn't understand why the best of people encounter the worst of situations relationally, physically, and in all other areas of life.

But one day, the Lord gave me a revelation of why we go through certain situations. Since receiving that revelation, I get a sense of joy, even when I get frustrated. Though I'm somewhat uncomfortable, I still have joy because I *know* why some of these things happen.

Peter tells us that we shouldn't be surprised when we suffer painful trials as though something *strange* has happened to us (1 Peter 4:12). We've heard this verse preached a million times, and we always think about the word *strange* with the connotation that relates to something being odd or weird or perplexing. But I researched the use of the word *strange.*

When Peter uses this word the second time, he means something foreign. We can relate the use of the word to the Old Testament when the Israelites were offering *strange* fire to the Lord. This meant that they were offering something foreign to the Lord. In relation to this use of the word *strange,* the Amplified Bible says "unusual and alien to you and your position."

This means that sometimes we encounter certain hardships and tragedies and immediately rebuke the devil because he's obviously coming against us and trying to deter us from God's blessing. Many of us have been praying for a promotion or a blessing, and we immediately come upon hard times.

Then we get upset and go into spiritual warfare because we're encountering something that's foreign to us and our position in God. But the Lord shared with me what really happens during a promotion.

The Bible tells us that God's ways are not our ways, neither are His thoughts ours (Isaiah 55:8). Therefore, we can't have a human perspective when approaching the things of God. God's definition of promotion is not the world's definition of promotion. God's promotion moves the believer forward. *Pro-* means forward, and when coupled with *motion* we get a clearer understanding of what happens during a God-promotion.

With every God-promotion, the believer realizes, receives, experiences, and lives in more and more of God's version of reality for their lives. Promotion is walking into more of the Word spoken over our lives. And we know that God's

Word is *spirit and life* (John 6:63). When we begin to walk in His Word and His Word becomes what frames our lives, the natural or carnal things of the world tend to disappear.

Oftentimes, in order to really train us to receive His Word, which is *spirit*, for our lives, God must shape our situation so that we can rely *only* on those things that are *spirit*. This is a promotion into another level of walking in God's Word and receiving His destined plan for our lives. The world says cutback, but God has said promotion. Friends have left, but God says promotion. Isolation equals promotion; financial challenges may mean promotion. Actually, these hardships don't point to promotion—they are, in fact, a promotion within themselves.

With every difficulty, the flesh dies. When the flesh dies—the spirit thrives and the whole man steps into more of God's reality. Our flesh begins to die as we submit more and more of our will and our lives to God. We begin to depend on Him more wholly because our situation drives us into prayer and we begin to learn more about God's faithfulness.

God's not hiding our promotion from us! Our promotion is not hidden on the other side of this struggle. We've been looking for the wrong thing! We've been calling the promise (the product or final end) the promotion. And we've been calling the promotion the pain, problem, and penalty. These are promotions—forward motion into the promise!

The flesh must die before you receive the promise, Abram. Promotion does not come from the east or the west (Psalm 75:6). It's nothing we can see with our carnal eyes. It comes from the Lord. As a matter of fact, we don't know what to look for because we've accepted the world's definition of promotion. We're looking for a pay increase, a new car, and a corner office, but we're getting more obstacles, car problems, and persecution on the job. But nevertheless, *rejoice!* Take joy in knowing what the Lord is doing in your life.

These momentary afflictions are teaching you that you can't rely on flesh and blood to receive what you need in this life. You've got to get it from God. That's why they're called fiery trials. He has sent His refiner's fire to purge us of dead works and dead thinking.

But if we don't realize it's Him doing these things, we'll fall by the wayside, thinking that we'll always be defeated. But once we realize that part of what we go through is making us better equipped to handle the promise that God has made us, we'll begin to rejoice. We have now become aware of God's work in our lives.

We're blessed, and the enemy can't curse what God has blessed. When Balak, the king of Moab, called on a soothsayer named Baalam to curse God's people, Baalam couldn't do it (Numbers 22 and 23)! He tried three times to curse them, but God wouldn't allow it, because they were His people. And if God is blessed, then His people, who are in divine covenant with Him, are blessed too. Baalam wanted to curse the people, but God would not let him. He wouldn't allow it then, and He won't allow it now!

> *With every difficulty, the flesh dies. When the flesh dies—the spirit thrives.*

The enemy can't curse what God has blessed! But our attitude can detain us! Once Baalam found out that he couldn't get to God's people, he tried to draw God's people away from Him! We are so powerful that each of us represents one of the two people that have a say-so over our destiny. The other person is God, and we already know how He feels. So get a perspective on what God has done in your life and don't let the seen hardships of life fool you into thinking that God will not fulfill His words of promotion to you.

Yes, it's uncomfortable, and what you've gone through may appear to indicate that God has forsaken you. But a promise is a promise. Begin to get in God's presence and find out what He says about your situation. Whatever He says will be. He's just making you better able to handle it when it comes to pass. So *rejoice!*

Praise God, you've received your promotion. It didn't come from the east or the west. You didn't detect it or time its coming like you can time the setting and the rising of the sun. You have to rely on the *Son* and His covenant with you for this one. God is just making it easy for you to receive your promotion. You can't rely on the things, people, and ways of the world anymore; He's made sure of that.

You've just been promoted—you've begun forward, positive motion into God's destiny for your life. The only way out is HIM, and that's just the way He likes it.

So, if the heat has been turned up in your life, shout YES! Let these fiery trials fulfill their purpose and burn away the carnal areas of your life. When His glorious fruit is revealed in you, you'll be thankful for the pain and suffering you endured for that short time. Your fruit will now remain because you have the joy that produces the strength to take on more of the weight of glory that God has brought into your life.

"Whether you're on TV, or whether you're in the office working, somebody's life is depending on you being the representative that you're supposed to be. Somebody's depending on you to go through the fire with a smile. And people need to see Jesus."

CeCe Winans

Part 3

◖◉ Much Fruit ◉◗

Prayer & Praise Power

"The issue is not whether I'm fruitful or not. Because I am—without a doubt! The issue is whether or not I know how I got here. I've got skills, true enough. But I can't forget where my real help comes from!"

These chapters would be incomplete without a nod at how we really get to the place called "there" in our search for purpose, fulfillment, and destiny. It is true; God has done some great things in our lives, but it's been through the direction we've received while being in God's presence that has made all of the difference.

Look Toward the Light!

Isaiah 60: 1–2; Psalm 23: 4–5

HAVE YOU EVER BEGUN A DAY that was so similar to so many other days that you were confused about exactly which day it really was? The kids were doing their morning routines, your spouse was rushing to begin the day's activities, the dog barked at exactly the same time, and the paper hit the door at its regularly scheduled moment.

Like the movie with Bill Murray, it was a day like yesterday, and the day before that.

As you wandered through this "Groundhog Day" of events, you were awake, but what you needed was a spiritual awakening. Life certainly can seem to be mundane, but there comes a time when the same ol' same ol' just won't do anymore. So, stop!

Stop right where you are and declare that your day will not be a day like any other. It's your time! Your light has come and the glory of the Lord has risen upon you (Isaiah 60: 1–2).

In order for us to bear spiritual fruit, we need this light. No plant, no fruit, and no tree grows without the right amount of light. If we're not careful, we'll allow the darkness of our human world to overshadow the light and glory of the Lord. School shootings, kidnappings, and terrorism will cloud our thoughts, hinder our faith, and inhibit our ability to let heaven's light shine on us.

Yes, the world is dark, and the human race is even darker. But you're a child of God. And you are a candidate for His bright glory to appear over you. Your Light, the Light of the World, has come. He wants to shine His light through you. That's right; you've been specially chosen to show that you've been brought out of darkness into His marvelous light (1 Peter 2:9).

So if you want to bear fruit, you must get some Son! Spend some time with the One whose overpowering light pierces the darkness. Whatever went wrong, even if it's your fault, just know that your Light has come, and with Him, things can only get better.

There is a miracle in the Light, even when your world seems dark. You may be experiencing some very dark days. Everything around you may be radiating darkness. Your earthly relationships may be unstable, your faith may be wavering, and your confidence in God and yourself may be plummeting. There may be many decisions you need to make, yet your pathway seems so dreary.

If you're feeling this way, your circumstances may be very real, but you may be looking at an illusion. The shadows of death may have clouded the truth. But there's help for you! It's time for you to learn the truth. Did you know that the Word of God is truth? The Lord told His people in Malachi 2:6 that the covenant He had with Levi caused those he influenced to walk in truth. Well, Levi is not the only person who has a covenant with God. Every believer has a covenant with God, signed in the blood of Jesus, and that covenant says that we've been redeemed from the curse of the law. Through Him, we have a right to the tree of life, and abundant life—on this side of heaven!

But we've got to walk in the right path. When the view of our path is clouded, there's only one thing we can do. We've got to find out what God says about our situation, in His Word and to us personally. We can make it, when we find out the truth through His Word.

We get the Word through study, prayer, and personal relationship with God, and we get the Word through the men and women God has sent into our lives. We need the Word in all of these ways. When we receive God's

Word for our lives, we find that it will serve as a lamp for our feet and a light for our path (Psalm 119:105). We'll not only be able to see where we are in God's plan for our lives, but we'll be able to see the roadblocks and obstacles on our path clearly.

Have you ever gotten a pebble in your shoe? Well, when you feel it in your shoe, many times you're convinced that it is a huge stone. But when you actually see it, you almost laugh because it is so small you can hardly pick it up with two fingers.

> *If you want to bear fruit, you must get some Son!* ⋙

Sometimes, that's just how life is. Life throws a little pebble in our shoe, but it feels like a gigantic boulder. It's when we receive revelation through the light of God's Word that we find out what we thought were huge rocks were glorified, magnified grains of sand. And those pebbles are often distractions on our path. While we're busy concentrating on life's teeny, tiny issues, we can fall into quicksand, make a wrong turn off of a cliff, or walk straight into a booby trap.

But the light of God's Word shows us truth; it helps us on our pathway to destiny, and helps nourish the growing fruit in our lives. Sometimes we don't know which path to take because we simply cannot see the road! Knowing what the Word says about you and your situation will clear up your vision and dispel the darkness that surrounds you.

Remember, we can't limit our definition of the Word to the written words in the Bible. We have to know what the Living Word is saying, and the Living Word is Jesus Christ (John 1:1,14). Not only is He God's Son, but He's "chock full" of grace and truth.

Not only that, when He ascended into heaven, He sent His Spirit, the Spirit of Truth, to live within us.

So the question is: do you know Jesus? And if you've only met Him, have you allowed Him, in His eternal power, to show you the truth about your situation? He can and He will. So what are you waiting for? Walk in the Light! He's the Living Light, ready to show you the way to victory and success. As a matter of fact, He *is* the way, the truth, and the life. He's the

Light of the world and He's waiting to dispel the cloudiness of your situation. After all, those things in your situation are the most temporary "elements" in your life. But the light inside of you lives forever.

Don't let your circumstances block your view! Look toward the Light!

You Won't Beat Me Praising God for My Blessing!

Psalm 95:6–11; Exodus 15, 17–18

WE'VE ALL HEARD THE FAMILIAR VERSE of scripture: "weeping endures for a night, but joy comes in the morning" (Psalm 30:5). There are wonderful stories that illustrate the significance of having a great morning after toiling through a horrendous night.

Jacob wrestled with the angel of the Lord all night until he received his blessing at daybreak. Paul and Silas were imprisoned and began to sing praises to God; and at the very beginning of the next morning, the prison doors were miraculously opened.

We've praised the Lord for all of these miraculous stories, but what did we do when we finally woke to our own personal victorious mornings? Psalm 95 speaks of the Lord and all of His greatness, and it instructs us to worship the Lord our Creator. Then, it would seem that the mode of the whole psalm shifts and the Lord begins to speak of the Israelites and their behavior after God delivered them from Egypt.

163

Did you know that the children of Israel fought and quarreled with Moses (and, ultimately, with God) during their wilderness experience? God had divided the Jordan River while Pharaoh and his army drowned in it. God had fed them bread from heaven. He had even cooled them by day and warmed them by night. At every obstacle, the Lord provided a remedy to their situation. But it was never good enough.

They were satisfied for a short time, but they questioned God's ability to lead them into the Promised Land. But here's what's worse. When Jethro, Moses' father-in-law, heard of all the wonderful things the Lord had done for the ungrateful children of Israel, He rejoiced and offered sacrifices to the Lord.

He only *heard* of the miracles that God had performed and, based solely on what he heard, said, "Now I know that the Lord is greater than all gods." He wasn't even there and his faith was strengthened and he praised the Lord!

For that matter, we weren't even there and we use that story as a point of reference for all that God can do. It's possible that more people have praised the Lord for what He did for the Israelites than the Israelites themselves.

When they first crossed the Red Sea, Moses sang and Miriam sang and played the tambourine in celebration of what God had done for them. Their enemies had drowned in the sea after trying to pursue God's Chosen people. And though they celebrated, sang, and danced, by the end of the same chapter, they were already grumbling because they had tasted bitter water (Exodus 15:24). Their grumbling continued, sometimes about food, other times about the journey they had to take.

They could have chosen to continue to praise God for what He had done for them. But by the second month of their journey toward freedom, they cried out for the familiar slave amenities of leeks, onions, and hard work.

Moses replied to their grumbling with soothing words, assuring the people that God would rain down bread and meat from heaven. By these miracles, they would know that God had been faithful in bringing them out of Egypt—as if God needed to prove Himself to them again!

He had drowned an entire army in the Red Sea while He parted that same sea with a strong wind so they could cross through it (Exodus 14:21). Did God need to prove another thing to them?

Sometimes, that's just how we are. We forget to use what God has done for us as a point of reference for all that He will continue to do for us as we journey to our own personal Promised Land. That journey can be trying, but we have to realize that after being rescued from tragic circumstances, we are not entirely prepared to walk immediately into the fullness of what God has promised us. We must endure the process of walking into our final destination of fulfilled dreams.

At every obstacle, the Lord provided a remedy to their situation. But it was never good enough. ☙

This truth becomes only more glaringly obvious as Moses coaxes the Israelites to closely follow God's ordinances during the following years. As the great Jehovah Jireh begins to provide manna, daily bread, for the children of Israel, Moses tells them that, with the exception of the Sabbath, they may only gather and eat the bread they received that morning—*that morning* (Exodus 16:16–20)! But they don't even heed these simple instructions. They attempt to keep the manna overnight, only to discover that it has spoiled and bred worms.

And when Moses tells them that on the sixth day they should gather enough manna for two days because the Sabbath is the following day, and there would be no manna to gather that day, the children of Israel *still* go out to look for manna on the seventh day!

I am convinced that this is what having an ungrateful heart will do. When the Israelites stopped praising God for His redemptive work, they also forgot who He was, and more importantly, who He was to them! That's just what praise does. When we speak well of God, we aren't just thanking Him for all that He's done; we're reminding ourselves just how great, awesome, and faithful He is!

Furthermore, we really can't speak of God's mighty acts as we're told to in Psalm 150 without remembering just how powerful He is. Had the children of

Israel forgotten about the ten plagues God had sent upon the people of Egypt, while He still sustained them? God does so much on our behalf that we become spoiled and ungrateful, acting as though God *must* do things our way! We forget that we've misbehaved enough to merit the visitation of some plagues of our own! Truly, it pays to stay on God's good side!

Developing a heart of praise and worship keeps a cycle of blessing and deliverance going in our lives. It's not quite as simple as the saying, "When praises go up, blessings come down," as if God reacts solely to our flattery. God does so many things for us despite what we do or say to Him or about Him. The truth is, when we praise the Lord, we leave room, by way of our mentality, for Him to act in our circumstances.

Remember, we've been made in His image, so we have a certain amount of power to change our circumstances by speaking life or death (Proverbs 18:21). Our mouths can frame our worlds, and when we praise God, we remind ourselves that He really is able to do great things for us. We speak positively about our situations and struggles, and they begin to change. And the part of our circumstances that we can't change, we have power, through praise, to allow God a place in our lives to change us and them!

Praise and worship is part of what allows God this place in our lives. Remember, God dwells in the praises of His people (Psalm 22:3). So when we give Him what we owe Him—praise—He makes a dwelling place among us. He sets up camp right where we are! And when He comes, He brings the characteristics and virtue that we need from Him. God is so giving that when you give Him something as simple as pure, unadulterated, innocent, and untainted praise, His character won't allow Him to be selfish. His presence alone radiates joy, pleasures, and virtue that we need for our present circumstances.

This is the cycle that ensues when we praise God. So why would anyone want to stop praising Him when, first of all, He deserves it, and secondly, we benefit from it! And certainly no one else should show more gratitude for what we've received from God, but we grumble to ourselves about what else isn't going right! Could it be we've stopped the cycle of what God wants to do in our lives?

The reality is that God took the children of Israel the route that He did, though it was a bit longer, because if He took them the shortest way, they would have faced war with the Philistines, given up, and gone back to slavery (Exodus 13:17). God knows what's best for us, and while we grumble, we should thank Him, because He is allowing us to take certain paths in our lives that may not seem to be the easiest ones, but they are the best ones. He knows our minds, and He knows our tendency to give up. And He knows how much we can bear (1 Corinthians 10:13)!

So through all of the changes, transitions, and inconveniences, we have a responsibility to keep an "attitude of gratitude" not just for what the Lord has already done for us but for the wisdom (that we may not even understand) that He employs in guiding us through our present difficulties.

Has God done something so awesome for you that it astonished others, and yet your praise only lasted a short while before you started crying out for leek sandwiches and onion gravy? Are people who weren't even there to personally witness God's miracle-working power rejoicing over your blessing more than you are? Sometimes, we've been in a dark night for so long, that we fail to believe that it really is morning when it dawns in our lives. We expect the sun to fall from the sky so that the familiar darkness can take its place in our lives again. Or, we complain and treat God like He's a magician who must pull another rabbit out of the hat before we believe He'll do all that He promised us.

But my friend, I'll tell you what I sometimes have to remind myself of. Your blessing, no matter how big or small, was the first step toward your destiny. No, the Lord didn't take you from bondage and drop you immediately into your promised land, but that doesn't mean you'll never make it there. It just means that God is still preparing you so that when you walk into your final destination, you'll be able to handle the great weight and responsibility that a blessing of that magnitude brings.

But whatever your destiny, and whatever the blessing you receive on the way to the Promised Land, don't let *anyone* beat you praising God for it!

So it's your turn; you've asked God to make you a fruitful person. Well, start by praising Him for the fruit that He's already brought to bear in your life. Praise Him for *all* that He's doing in your life—great and small! Canaan's just around the corner; you'll be there in no time!

River of Life

John 7:37–39

HAVE YOU EVER JUST HAD one of *them days?* The *them days* are days where nothing is necessarily wrong, but something just isn't right. You may not even be able to put your finger on it, but your emotional state has caused you to be physically exhausted, your spirit seems to be parched, and your soul is gasping for air.

I've had one of them days one too many times, and I've found a great remedy. When everything inside me seems to be drying up, and I seem to find no physical or emotional solution, I've found that Jesus has supplied a river of life that's longing to come flowing out of me. The river that Jesus refers to in John 7:37–39 is the Holy Spirit, and anytime the dry and barren circumstances of life seem to cause my spirit to shrivel up, I've got just the source of water to satisfy any deficiency.

I am so thankful for the Holy Spirit. I'm thankful, not because I can brag that I have Him while I make others feel jealous or inferior because they don't. I'm grateful that I have a Divine Helper abiding on the inside of me that lives and loves to make intercession for me (Romans 8:26).

And on a day like this—He's just what I need. The demands of my job are great, and actually things are going well. It's an exciting time professionally, per-

168

sonally, and spiritually. I'm accomplishing more than I'd ever dreamed I would, and I've experienced the grace and mercy of God more than I'd ever thought I would, could, or should. I feel as if, at any moment, great and wonderful things are going to happen to me, through me, and for me. That's right—I'm the one who can run through troops and leap over walls. I've grown in my walk with God, and He's certainly proved to be my greatest resource and asset. People who love me, care for me, and appreciate me surround me.

So why am I feeling the way that I am?

It would seem as if everything is looking up for me—and, for the most part, everything is. I have a reason to celebrate, and even in the midst of celebration, deep down on the inside, there's something going on—my mind is burdened, my heart is heavy—and even though I'm on the verge of a breakthrough, I'm also on the brink of a meltdown.

It's funny how we celebrate the wrong things. Like I said, sometimes, there can be nothing wrong outwardly; as a matter of fact, things seem to be going well. It's my party and there's plenty to eat and drink, yet it's on the inside that I'm so thirsty...

That's what it must've been like in John 7. It was the Feast of Tabernacles. The Feast of Tabernacles was a seven-day celebration that would remind the people of Israel that God brought them out of Egypt and made places for them to live, and for Him to live among them. This feast occurred after the Day of Atonement, when the people were reminded of their sins, and made sacrifices to God for them. These feasts are symbolic acts that show us a greater spiritual truth. The people had made provisions to be absolved of their sins, and now they were celebrating the opportunity to live apart from enslavement—of people and of sin.

Around verse 37 of John 7, Jesus exclaims: "If any man is thirsty, let Him come to me and drink!"

Well, hold up Jesus! Aren't we at the final and greatest day of a feast? Shouldn't there be plenty to eat *and* drink? How can it be that at my own party, I can't get what I really need to drink? After all the great things that are going on in my life, I've got a reason to celebrate. The people had celebrated the forgiveness they had received through their sacrifices of atonement. Now they were celebrating the chance to live in God's presence free from bondage.

But I suspect that after performing these rituals year after year, their perspective on these rites changed, and the celebrations became more about what they'd done to receive gifts of forgiveness and freedom from God, rather than what God had done for them.

We celebrate our own accomplishments and that's nice. But there's something about celebrating the One who empowers you to do great things. Jesus put it this way earlier in the same chapter: "He who speaks on his own does so to gain honor for himself, but he who works for the honor of the one who sent him is a man of truth; there is nothing false about him" (John 7:18 NIV).

> *Take your mind off of your selfish pursuits and accomplishments and put it on Him.* ☽

Sometimes we feel so depleted and empty, even though everything is going our way. But we're experiencing a drought in our spirits because so much of what we say and do selfishly relates to ourselves. That's when the *them days* set in.

Am I the only one who's experienced this? I doubt it. Am I the only one who's found a way to cope with this feeling? That's doubtful, as well. But let me tell you what's worked for me: praying in the Spirit.

When Jesus made His bold proclamation that anyone who comes to Him could drink and never thirst again, He then described the Holy Spirit as a river of living water. It is when the Holy Spirit is inside of you that a refreshing takes place, quenching the thirsty soul. And praying in the Spirit helps quench the recurring thirst that occurs in our lives.

You see, when everything on the outside seems to be just a-okay, but on the inside there's turmoil, you need relief. Seemingly, you have no reason to complain or be anxious. Things are going well, and only getting better. But when issues, struggles, and even silly mental burdens threaten your performance or just threaten to ruin your day—you've got to take control.

Sometimes, you may not even be able to diagnose the reason for your uneasiness—although many times you *are* able to, and just don't want to admit what the real problem is. Either way, praying in the Spirit does several things for the Spirit-filled believer. Here's just one.

Romans 8:26–27 states that when we don't know what to pray for, the Holy Spirit takes up the slack for our unawareness. Do you know that we're not commanded to know everything about every situation? Sometimes, the Christian world pressures us into thinking that just because we've been saved, filled, thrilled, and chilled by *He* who knows all things, *we* must know all things as well. Well, what need would we have for the gifts of salvation or the Holy Spirit if once we received them, we didn't need any more supernatural assistance?

Salvation is not just a one-time purchase that we pick up at the five-and-dime. It's a gift, and true salvation is the gift that keeps on giving. It never stops making provisions for us. Salvation is active, continually allowing us spiritual access to spiritual solutions for life's continuous challenges. Salvation is for this world, and the world to come. We'll always need the gift that Jesus gave us through His death. And while we're here on earth, we'll always need the Comforter that Jesus sent to the earth to help us when He ascended to heaven. We need help!

We've received salvation, but we haven't accessed all the power and benefits that come with it. Today, sometimes it seems as though the only way to be considered a true Christian is to join the Christian band of people who feign instant and complete healing and restoration from everything that has ever ailed them physically, emotionally, and spiritually. The moment we became saved, we had to have it absolutely and completely "together."

This "I've-got-it-all-together" mentality is what causes secret sins to remain secret and hidden fears to fester. Both give the enemy power to work in our lives. Meanwhile, we're deceived into believing that because we've been blood-bought, we're now card-carrying devil-busters that have personally conquered death, hell, and the grave. We have actually made a carnal and mental blunder—we've exalted ourselves to a role of god-hood.

Rather than being kings and priests ruled by the King of kings and the High Priest, we've tried to assume His position at the right hand of the Father. We've tried to be everyone's savior, healer, and deliverer, when we're supposed to point them to He who is everyone's Savior, Healer, and Deliverer. We feel guilty when we fail at these roles, not ever realizing that we're trying to fill some very big shoes.

Listen, friend. Take your mind off of your selfish pursuits and accomplishments and put it on Him. We are only the body functioning from the all-knowing mind and headship of Christ Jesus. What body still operates effectively without the head in place? Jesus is our Head; He's the system of control. Don't cut Christ's headship from your spiritual equation—you'll be just like a chicken with its head cut off. You'll be running this way and that, but you'll never go anywhere—but to the deep fryer of despair! Though you'll be at the table, and you'll most definitely be in the presence of your enemies, you won't be served a feast—you'll be served *as* the feast!

You won't win any battles, nor gain any spoils if you don't let God be God in your life. You'll never be truly victorious until you submit to your power source for guidance in this Christian journey.

So what does this have to do with praying in the Spirit? I'm glad you asked. Keep reading.

The Power of the Hook-Up

⟪ *John 14* ⟫

JAMES 3 TELLS US JUST HOW POWERFUL, and yet how untamed, our tongue is. It is a little fire, but can ignite huge disasters in our lives! We often use the same tongue to bless God and to curse our enemies, and even our friends. James says something very important about what comes out of our mouths. James 3:2–3 tells us that if we can keep from causing trouble with our mouths, we can direct our bodies. We can turn our circumstances around! We can keep from walking down the wrong road! We can do all of this with our tongues!

Now we can do a certain amount of this by meditating on the Word of God, even though there are some situations in which we don't even know what Scripture to quote. There are some issues that may not even allow us the time to research what classic Bible story corresponds to the situation. We are to study the Word and keep it in our mouths, but God does not expect us to know His written Word while we don't take advantage of His Living Word! He is so good to us! He knows that we won't ever know everything about Him or His Word, but He sent us Someone who does!

In John 7:38–39, Jesus compared the Holy Spirit with a river of living water. Jesus promised us that He would come. In John 14:16–20, He also makes reference to the Comforter who would come and abide with us forever. It is through that Comforter that the disciples would know that Jesus is in His Father, and that we are in Him, and *He* would be in *us* (John 14:20). The Holy Spirit is not at all spooky. We use the terms Holy Spirit and Holy Ghost interchangeably, but we often use them incorrectly. Any time someone starts running and jumping in the church, we say, "Oh, Sister Lucy got the Holy Ghost in church this morning" as if she gets *IT* sporadically. Well, the Holy Spirit is not an *IT*. *It* is really a *Him*. He is Jesus' Spirit coming to us as a gift from God the Father.

Jesus said that when we receive the Holy Ghost, we have absolute proof that He is in us. Well, I thought the Holy Ghost was in us; He is. The Holy Ghost is Jesus' Spirit in us. Here's more scriptural proof. In Acts 1:1–2, Luke opens the book telling us that his purpose of writing was to tell what Jesus said and did before He ascended into heaven. Then he makes a powerful statement in verse 2: "After that [Jesus' ascension] he *through* the Holy Ghost had given commandments unto the apostles whom he had chosen" (emphasis mine). Wait! Does this mean that Jesus now operates through the Holy Ghost? Yes, that's exactly what this means.

Many of us are falsely indoctrinated into thinking that we'd be some strange specimens if we even so much as claimed to have the Holy Spirit. But the fact of the matter is that Jesus said that our having the Holy Spirit is proof that He's with His Father, and we're in Him and He's in us. He is literally in us, through the Holy Spirit! That's why the Holy Spirit isn't an *it!* The Holy Ghost is God's Spirit on the inside of us.

Simply put, when the Holy Spirit is inside of you, you are now part of a Divine Hookup! Jesus is in God, we're in Jesus (thus the term *Christians*, meaning "of and like Christ"), and He's in us through His Spirit. The Bible says that a three-fold cord is not easily broken (Ecclesiastes 4:12), meaning that there's strong, undeniable unity when three gather together. The Holy Spirit, especially in His active state, places us at the table with the Masterminds and CEOs of the universe. With them living in us, the same power they have is made available to us.

Here's the key: we're not really part of the three-fold cord! John 14:23 tells us that if we honor Jesus' words, His commandments, and His teaching concerning the Holy Spirit, He and the Father would come to us and make the dwelling with us. How do they make their dwelling? Through our obedience to the Holy Spirit!

The Holy Spirit brings the entire Blessed Trinity to us! We're not the third part of the power cord; we are the vehicles in which they abide and we're the conduits in which they flow. The Living Water comes out of us, showing the glory of the Lord. The bottom line is this: God wants to use you, and in order to operate at the optimal capacity designed for your life, you need the Holy Spirit at work.

> *The Holy Spirit, especially in His active state, places us at the table with the Masterminds and CEOs of the universe.*

Many of us study the book of Acts and know that toward the beginning of the book the Holy Spirit came to the world. We've read Acts 2 and have been convinced that speaking in tongues, also called praying in the spirit, was only meant for those particular people in the upper room. But to discount praying in the Spirit is to discount that Jesus is in us, and that we're in Him and that He's in His Father.

Throughout the end of John 14, Jesus stresses keeping His words and commands, not just because we can't serve two masters, but because we must also honor this particular teaching about the Holy Spirit in order to walk in the destiny God has prepared for us. To deny the Holy Spirit license to flow in your life as a river of Living Water is to deny Jesus permission to fully work through you and operate *in you*. The Holy Spirit within us is Jesus in God, and we in Jesus.

I don't know about you, but I don't want to *not* be in Christ Jesus. The Bible says that if any man be in Christ, he's a new creature and that old things have passed away and that all things have become new (2 Corinthians 5:17). If I'm not in Him, I can't have this new life. But it starts with the understanding that to be in Him means that His Spirit, the Holy Spirit, must be in us. When the

Holy Spirit is in us, the triune being of God is in us, and we'll be able to do the greater works Jesus spoke about in John 14:12. The greater works are available to us because Jesus said He was going to be with His Father and then they would all come to be within us. But we've got to receive His teaching about the Holy Spirit.

Perhaps that's why we often don't see the *new life* come to real fruition in our lives in every area. We've been fooled into thinking that the baptism of the Holy Spirit is only for fanatics, that it's for a club of people who jump, shout, shuck, and jive.

But the real baptism in the Holy Spirit is about Jesus. It's about having access to His Spirit. It really meant something to the apostles to have His Spirit within them, because they had *Him* with them for so long. They needed Jesus' Spirit to continue the work that began in them while He was with them.

We've never had the physical Jesus with us, so the baptism of the Holy Spirit seems a bit more removed from us. I truly believe that's what causes *them days.* We feel so dried up, and God seems to be so far from us. It's because our contact with Jesus is not what it should be. Even believers who already have received the baptism of the Holy Spirit have *them days.* We need a refreshing, and it all comes through our tongue. We don't know it all, yet we have the power of death and life at work in us through our tongues.

I believe that's why when God sent the Holy Spirit, the first thing that was affected was the tongue. The Holy Spirit is like the bit that James said is put in the mouth of a horse that causes the horse to turn about, resulting in the turning of the whole body (James 3:3). The path of our life will change, and the way in which we travel through it will change when we begin to actively understand what praying in the Spirit is all about.

There's been some bad representation of just what it means to be filled with the Holy Spirit with the evidence of speaking in other tongues. It's not for show, and it's not for arrogance. Receiving the baptism of the Holy Spirit demonstrates our submission to the Lord and His guidance, teaching, and leading into the path of truth. The truth that we know makes us free (John 8:32), but when we don't even know the truth about our lives and our situations, it's so good to know the Spirit of truth (John 14:17)!

Face it. Sometimes, we don't even know what to wear. How can we know what to pray for? The Holy Spirit relieves the pressure of having to figure every-thing out. Don't worry; you're still a man or woman of great faith and power! But your faith will be in your Savior, and your true power will come from sub-mitting your master controls to the One who has all power and knows all things.

Warning! You'll now be able to rest easier, and when life's problems come and pressures, explained or unexplained, arise, you have a way to employ the Spirit of God on your behalf. You don't have to know it all to get some help in this life! But you do have to be smart—smart enough to know that you can't handle all of the details of your life! You've got to be willing to submit your will and your tongue, and have an interface with the Holy Ghost that is out of this world, enabling you to conquer the trials that come in this world.

Just taking time to pray in the Spirit releases daily pressure and calms unex-plainable fears. It's so meaningful to know that I only have to make contact with the One who knows it all.

Be mindful; the Word of God tells us to be aware of the enemy's devices (2 Corinthians 2:11). Praying in the Spirit is not a substitute for praying with an understanding and seeking the face of God for wisdom about how to go about handling life's struggles. Neither is praying in the Spirit an excuse to close your Bible and not learn what was written in it. They all work hand in hand.

While we're on this side of eternity, we'll only know things in part, and we'll only understand life and the things of God in part, even after long hours of study. Praying in the Spirit helps release us from the ungodly responsibility of having to know it all. What we know, we articulate to Him in prayer. What we do not know, we allow the Holy Spirit to ease our uneasiness and then we rest, knowing He has solved our problems. We can be fruitful and we can mul-tiply! Those dry, shriveled up *them days* will turn into days of triumph as you experience rivers of living water that will leave you completely satisfied with a deeper level of relationship with the Lord.

Enough to Go Around

⊚ *John 14:26–28* ⊚

PEOPLE ARE SO NEEDY. In one way or another, we are all very needy. You may be saying, "I'm not needy! I don't need nothing or nobody!" Well, sir or ma'am, I don't believe you. I don't even believe that you believe you. Whether you realize it or not, you're needy too. I know I am.

I am the youngest in my family. So when I arrived on the scene, the house was already full, complete with extras. With parents, brothers, grandparents, uncles, and cousins around, I was *never* alone. *Never!* It never really bothered me at first because I have a way of disconnecting into my own world. Also, I had no other point of reference. I wasn't the oldest child or an only child from a small family who knew what it was like for the house to be quiet before all of "them" got there.

Nope, I was born "smack-dab" in the middle of a party—and many times I just *knew* that I was the guest of honor! Well, as I reached my teenage years, I can remember that there were times when I was ready for that party to be over!

"Stop the bus, please! I know I'll have to walk, but I'll do it, if I can just get some peace and quiet!"

I didn't really get the peace and quiet I had begun to crave until I was about sixteen. My brothers had moved out, and the other family members that were

178

around the house weren't around as much and—aah—do you hear that? That's right! It's the sweet sound of nothing! I can remember rushing home from school or my part-time job, relishing the thought of being home alone! Sometimes, I wouldn't even turn on the TV—and for this '80s TV kid, that's amazing! It was wonderful—peace and quiet.

Well, I'm needy, like I said. But I'm also wishy-washy. There were times I'd think, *Where's everybody at?* So I'd find some friends to go hang out with or just go run in the streets.

I was finally alone! And I didn't always like it. Can you imagine what the disciples felt like when Jesus started telling them He was going to have to go away, and leave them alone? During their short time with Him, they had faced some dangerous situations that may have made them want to return to their quiet lives of fishing, tax collecting, or doctoring. But in the final analysis, they really didn't like the thought of being without Jesus.

When He began to tell them that He was leaving, even the news that the Holy Spirit was coming in His place didn't seem to be enough. Here was this guy who did and said such great things, and was able to bail Himself out of tight jams—and now He says He's leaving?

Here was this guy who did and said such great things, and was able to bail Himself out of tight jams—and now He says He's leaving?

This must have really bothered His disciples, because Jesus had to have this conversation with them several times. And each time He mentioned His leaving, He had to soothe their anxiety about it. It reminds me of a parent who's going on a trip and keeps reminding the child that "Daddy's going out of town. You know you're going to have to stay with Auntie Ethel, but don't worry; I'll be back!"

Well, of course I'm worried. I love Auntie Ethel, but she's not my mama or daddy! Each time Jesus mentioned His imminent departure, it was as if He had to convince His children that it was good for Him to go, because He'd be bringing a gift back. He must have sensed their discomfort when He said,

"Peace I leave with you, my peace I give unto you: not as the world giveth, give I unto you. Let not your heart be troubled, neither let it be afraid" (John 14:27).

In John 16, the disciples still didn't like the idea because He still had to soothe them again, saying, "But because I have said these things unto you, sorrow hath filled your heart. Nevertheless I tell you the truth; it is expedient for you that I go away: for if I don't go away, the Comforter will not come unto you; but if I depart, I will send him unto you" (vss. 6–7).

Well, both you and I know that He was right! I'm glad that I didn't have to suffer the loss of Jesus like the disciples did. I believe one of the first things that the Holy Spirit had to do when He arrived at Pentecost was comfort those who still mourned the loss of Jesus. Can you imagine it? As magnetic a personality as you and I have, Jesus was probably the greatest person of all time to be around! They missed Him badly; you'd better believe that!

And though He came back in the form of the Holy Spirit, I'm sure it still took some getting used to. They couldn't see Him, John couldn't hold Him, and Peter couldn't see Him shoot him annoyed looks. But, I know they felt Him! And the power! Absolutely out of this world! It took some getting used to, and I know that they must have longed to see Him, but I know they found out something special about the Holy Spirit.

With Jesus' Spirit on the inside of them, there was *finally* enough to go around! Finally I don't have to wait for John to get out of the way so I can love on Him! I don't have to wait for Peter to finish getting rebuked to hear the rest of what Jesus has to say! Philip isn't asking any more dumb questions, and even if he is, there's still enough of Jesus to go around! And now, I don't have to go find Him when I need my miracle. I can have it when I need it because when He sees me, He sees His Spirit within me, and His blood covering me. It's really a great deal!

Thank you, Jesus for going away! You sent Your Spirit back to me, and now there's more than enough of You to go around! He is a comforter when I'm lonely. He's a helper when I'm needy, and He's a guide when I'm wishy-washy and can't decide what to do. If you don't know if you have this Holy Spirit, stop right now and let Him in! If you ask Jesus to fill you with the Holy Spirit until He overflows, He'll do it—NOW! It's no trick, and it's definitely not spooky.

No wonder the disciples were always shooing children and adults away from Jesus. They wanted Him all for themselves. And now you and I can have Him. We don't have to pull children off of His lap because we want our turn in His arms. We don't have to press through crowds just to touch Him. We have a different kind of press now. We must press through distractions, fear, guilt, and shame. We must take the time to press past busy schedules, family responsibilities, and church auxiliary meetings and have our personal moments with Jesus.

My job is demanding and I work with people all day long. So there are times that I still rush home for peace and quiet. But now, I'm not just rushing home for peace and quiet. I've got peace already, knowing He's with me. I'm rushing home to spend personal and intimate time alone with Jesus through His precious Holy Spirit. I'd write more, but now it's time for just you and Him.

You, too, can have a personal experience with Him; just pray this simple prayer:

Dear Lord Jesus,

You sent the Comforter back to live and dwell in us. Because You loved us so much and knew we would fall short without Your presence, You sent the Holy Spirit to operate in the earth through us, the ones You gave Your life for. We're the ones You decided to do Your many works through.

It's my desire to take advantage of Your special gift to me. Holy Spirit, I want You to be more than a well of living water in me. I want You to fill me until I overflow. I want to be a part of that river of living water. I know there is more than enough of You for me and the lives I will touch, as I flow in You.

Lord, use me as an instrument of Your service. Let Your Spirit rule and reign in my life to Your honor and glory. Jesus, baptize me in Your precious Holy Spirit. As I go down into

Your Spirit, let me rise up with the power that He gives and the evidence of His presence, by speaking in tongues. I bind the enemy from any hindrance in my ability to speak, in Jesus' name.

Thank You Lord for Your undying love that sent the Comforter to this earth for me. There is enough to go around and I thank You!

Amen

So go ahead, let the Holy Spirit be an active participant in your life. You'll never be the same!

*"We were created for God.
God was not created for us."*

Kirk Franklin

CONCLUSION

"So it's settled! I'm nothing without Him! I need Him in every area of this walk through life. He gave me purpose, helped me discover the purpose He gave me, and He helped me pursue it! I think I've finally figured it out... There's no me without Him."

HE IS my Purpose!

That I May Know Him

⟨⟨ *Philippians 3:10* ⟩⟩

I AM A PRODUCT OF MY GENERATION. I am a compilation of my childhood experiences, my socioeconomic, geographic, and cultural backgrounds. I am what's around me now and what I've been before. And as a product of my generation, I have subconsciously acquired some of the mindset that characterizes my generation.

I would say that anyone born after 1970 could identify with what I'm going to say. Actually, anyone born before may recognize what I'm about to say even more readily because the trait that describes my generation is probably not as much a part of their generational make-up, so they might be able to identify those characteristics that are not like them.

One trait in particular that characterizes my generation is the tendency to want a shortcut for everything. We've heard of the fast-food mentality, but I believe it encourages more than wanting to "have it my way." Not only does our generation want it our way, but we want to be exempt from any regular process for acquiring everything, and we don't want to be accountable for anything.

We want to encounter life just as we do a drive-thru window. We want a short line. We want to order what we want, how we want it. We want our

order fulfilled nearly immediately and perfectly prepared to our specifica-
tions. We want to pay a low price to someone who doesn't know our name
or need to know our name—and we don't want to know theirs either unless
we want to complain about the service they've rendered.

Now if you're like me, you want the drive-thru to stay open late, just in
case you want to munch on something in the middle of the night. I want the
store to stay open all night. It sounds silly, but it's true. For some reason, I
always get the craving for a Sonic slush either after Sonic has closed or seven
minutes before it does.

It's quite funny really. I want a Sonic slush on a regular basis, but can
never anticipate this regular craving. I find myself rushing out the door and
thinking, *Maybe tonight they'll stay open 'til 12:03.* I admit it. In the past, this has
been my practice almost three times a week.

"Can I make it, can I make it, can I make it? Aw shucks, they just
turned off the lights just as I came around the corner."

This is my generation. This is what many of us do. We have a self-centered
mentality wanting the world to revolve
around us. And in case the rules or guidelines don't match my plan, maybe they'll
bend the rules just for me.

This mode of thinking applies to
much more than fast-food restaurants.
And I have to admit it; I've been affected
by it. Actually, I once had a form of this
thinking in regards to my relationship with
Christ. We've all read the familiar passage:

> *I want to know Christ and the power of his resurrection and the fellowship of sharing in his sufferings.*
> *—Philippians 3:10*

I used to think to myself, *If this fellow-
ship-of-His-suffering thing gets to out of hand, I may
have to backslide.* Oh, so we get all the way to
the end of the book and you want to act shocked! You may not have thought
this particular thought, but you've thought some other crazy stuff in your life.
I can remember thinking, *All these saved folk get attacked too much—and they don't ever
seem to win. If that happens to me—I'm outta here! I'm not down for all of that!*

I figured I'd get attacked less if I made less of a stance for Christ and the things I truly believed in. Hey, I can still get a good job and obtain success; I kinda have it going on. Life will be more fun, I'll have less conviction when I do wrong, and if I kinda-sorta hop the fence, I'll face less opposition from the enemy. Immature, I know. I'd been influenced by the fast-food mentality of "Give me what I want and let me be on my way. I want success with a side of happy times—and please—hold the trials and tribulation. Oh yeah, and give me one of those slushes too!" I wanted just enough of God to say grace over my food and know it worked.

Now, I'm happy to report that, by the grace of God, I don't have this mentality about my walk with Christ (though I still wish Sonic were open later!). Let me tell you some of what the Lord told me about it.

So many Christians have experienced suffering for one reason or another. It may have been self-imposed or they may have encountered hard times through no fault of their own. Sometimes, because we've been exposed to various hardships for so much of our lives, we'll do just about anything to have a time of peace and happiness in our life.

You may have once thought, *I never went through this when I was in the world!* Or *I was never attacked like this until I started going to this church! I never encountered this struggle until I started pursuing my call to ministry.*

You may have decided to give up and return to business as usual—this God-thing was more than you bargained for. Well, I'm not going to feed you a bunch of "church-isms" like "you've come too far to turn around," (though you have) or "trouble don't last always" (though it really doesn't). I'm just going to give you the Word of God.

We have to realize some things. First, the Bible says that in life, rain falls on the just and the unjust (Matthew 5:45). Bad things happen to good and bad people. No matter which side of the fence you're on, you won't escape problems. That's life.

You must also know that Ecclesiastes 3 tells us that to everything, there's a season. It didn't say, for every believer there's a season. *Everything* has a season. We'll all have seasons of life and death, good and bad, weeping and laughing. So if this season has gotten the best of you, hang in there.

The good thing about seasons is that they change. Circumstances change—and if your circumstance doesn't seem to be changing, change your perspective on the circumstance. The wise writer of Ecclesiastes goes on to tell us in 3:9–11 that those who struggle and work hard in the kingdom—despite seasonal shifts—will see that God will make all things beautiful in its time. That means that in everything—your life, your marriage, and your relationships with God and man—there is a preset time for it to become beautiful. Our requirement is to stay steadfast and unmovable, always abounding in the work of the Lord (1 Corinthians 15:58).

We have to know that neither our labor nor our hardships are in vain and that sooner or later, the season will change. After all, it is God's will for us to be happy. Ecclesiastes 3:13 tells us that it is God's gift for us eat, drink, and enjoy the fruit of our labor. This applies to physical food and drink and our occupations and jobs, but I also believe the meaning is a bit deeper than that.

I believe that this passage tells us that we will work, toil, and travail spiritually and emotionally, but after we've overcome it, God allows us to be nourished, refreshed, and fulfilled because we've been tenacious enough to work through our struggles.

We're nourished by our trials, and they give us strength to keep fighting and drive us to keep seeking God. During the different seasons of life, we truly become acquainted with the Lord. The hard times allow us to fellowship with Him, even as He suffered for our sake. Times of death and separation only allow us to know just how much power He has to resurrect us. We gain the will to live and face another day.

We learn some things by divine revelation, but I'm quickly discovering that most things I learn from and about God are in midst of sad, lonely, and uncomfortable times of despair. But here's what I learned: the people who know their God will be strong and do exploits (Daniel 11:32).

Some translations of this use of the word *know* indicate that we learn about God from seeing Him, meaning we must see God at work not just in our progress but also in our pain, which is often used to progress us further into God's plan for us. I learn about Him in a deeply personal way because I cling to Him for solutions to those deep, personal problems that only He can resolve.

Because I know God intimately, through patience, time-investment, and obedience, I'll be able to do those great things that I've wanted to do. And with His help, it'll be much easier.

That's what being fruitful and multiplying is all about. In the first chapters of the book, I mentioned that there is no fruit without intimacy. The womb that holds our dreams must be fertilized by the seed of the Spirit of God. This happens in many ways, but mostly like it happens in animal life. Any mother who has given birth will tell you: *"The normal course and operations of life are abruptly interrupted, and everything becomes topsy-turvy, while all focus is on this "thing" growing on the inside of me. Meanwhile, life still goes on but it seems like my appetite has changed and all along, there's a steady buildup of pressure on the inside that lets me know that sooner or later, this turbulent time of what feels like war on the inside of me will soon come to bring forth one of the most beautiful things I've ever seen. It's a miracle, but like any doctor will tell you, it's the closest you've ever been to death. And when you lay eyes on this beautiful, splendid miracle, the pain that you went through during this long, laborious process is almost forgotten, but not quite. . ."*

That's just what it's like giving birth to your dreams, and it all started when you made that step to become intimate, to *know* God. And even though it takes time and pain to birth each dream He places inside of you, He makes every change and every pain you go through worth the wait, once you see the realization of your dreams.

So, I've decided not to run out on God. And I can't try and find a fast-food way to get through life's seasons. I realized that I couldn't pop my vision in the microwave and get it out in time to watch a DVD on my laptop. Besides, food heated in a microwave never stays warm. When it comes time for me to bear fruit, I want mine to remain. I don't want to continuously have to reheat it like a TV dinner, and I don't want to have to shovel it in my mouth while it's still hot. I want my fruit to remain, and I want to enjoy the aroma of my destiny and savor the flavor of my blessings.

Life seems so fast nowadays, and technology is so advanced, but some things are worth the wait. This process of getting to know Him is no different, and to tell you the truth, I'm enjoying it more and more each day. I'm learning: seasons change, but God doesn't; I'm better off getting to know Him the slow-roasted way.

He'll make my life beautiful—in His time.

> *"The people that do know their God shall be strong,*
> *and do exploits."*

> Daniel 11:32

COMING SOON

Personal worship music from Kenneth M. Mosley
Based on the breakthrough book
Be Fruitful & Multiply

For more information
Logon to **www.KennethMosley.com**

Printed in the United States
50940LVS00007B/28-39